Tal The Puranas and Itihaas

Retold by Daaji

Edited by
Purnima Ramakrishnan

Illustrated by
Gayatri Pachpande

RED PANDA

First published by Red Panda, an imprint of Westland Books, a division of Nasadiya Technologies Private Limited, in 2023

No. 269/2B, First Floor, 'Irai Arul', Vimalraj Street, Nethaji Nagar, Alapakkam Main Road, Maduravoyal, Chennai 600095

Westland, the Westland logo, Red Panda and the Red Panda logo are the trademarks of Nasadiya Technologies Private Limited, or its affiliates.

Text and illustration copyright © Heartfulness Institute

Heartfulness Education Trust, asserts the moral right to be identified as the author of this work.

ISBN: 9789357765596

10 9 8 7 6 5 4 3

The views and opinions expressed in this work are the author's own and the facts are as reported by them, and the publisher is in no way liable for the same.

All rights reserved

Book design by New Media Line Creations, New Delhi 110 062

Printed at Thomson Press (India) Ltd

No part of this book may be reproduced, or stored in a retrieval system, or transmitted in any form or by any means, electronic, mechanical, photocopying, recording, or otherwise, without express written permission of the publisher.

Contents

Introduction	V
1. The Birth of the Elephant God	1
2. In Pursuit of Freedom	6
3. One Fruit, Two Brothers	12
4. An Enchanted Pool and Five Brothers	16
5. Jada Bharata's Journey	22
6. Hanuman Shows Humility	27
7. An Unnatural Heaven	31
8. Shakuntala: A Love Story	35
9. Woman Power in the Treta Yug	40
10. Bhagiratha: An Adventure in Perseverance	44
11. An Epitome of Faith and Confidence	50
12. Moving on from Mistakes	55
13. Churning the Ocean of Milk	61
14. Imitation Is Not Emulation	68
15. The Fragrant Parijat Flowers	72

16. Who Are You? An Ant? Indra?	75
17. Many Aeons, Many Lives, Same Devotion	80
18. Krishna's Relationship with Wealth	84
19. Power of Pause and Poise	88
20. The Law of Karma Catches Up	93
21. May Noble Thoughts Come from Everywhere	98
22. A Head on Top of a Hill	104
23. The Unexpected Help	110
24. The King Who Knew He Would Die in Seven Days	116
25. Nala Damayanti: A Beautiful Love Story	120

Introduction

My dear friends,

As a child, I was captivated by magical tales of gods and demons, warriors and wise people, the timid and brave, and good and evil. It amazes me how many of these stories, from my childhood and ancient scriptures, are still as vibrant and relevant today for the new generation.

For me, *The Tales from the Vedas and Upanishads*, with twenty-five fascinating tales from the ancient scriptures, was an exciting adventure into the heart's wisdom. And this collection of timeless stories, *The Tales from the Puranas and Itihaas*, is a natural extension, to inspire moral, ethical and spiritual values in young readers.

These tales from the Puranas and Itihaas, explore the rich tapestry of Indian mythology and spiritual landscape.

The word 'Purana' means ancient or old. The Puranas comprise ageless stories, myths and legends about the creation and destruction of the universe, the history and origins of gods, sages, the first man, his royal descendants and more. These stories may or may not be true, but the inspiration received from them is valuable for individual, national and global happiness and prosperity.

There are eighteen Mahapuranas or Puranas written by Veda Vyasa. Each Purana celebrates a specific god, just like *Vishnu Purana* is centred around Vishnu and the *Shiv Purana* around Shiva. Then there are the Upa-Puranas or the lesser important Puranas and the Sthala-Puranas that revolve around a sacred place.

'Iti haas' means 'it happened thus'. These stories are written by the one who was part of the story. Valmiki, who brought up Lord Rama's children, wrote the Ramayana. Veda Vyasa, the grandfather of Pandavas and Kauravas, wrote the Mahabharat. They are historical and even some archaeological evidence found in Dwaraka, Kurukshetra,

Panchavati in Nashik, and the Ram Sethu bridge connecting India to Sri Lanka, etc, to corroborate their validity.

But before we delve deeper into the stories of the Puranas and Itihaas, I want to take you all on an exploratory journey into your minds. Our planet's lost civilisations date back to only a few thousand years ago, and are still in this current cycle of time. But the ancient Indian scriptures discuss cycles of time, spanning four *yugs*:

1. Satya Yug (lasted 4,320,000 years)
2. Treta Yug (lasted 1,296,000 years)
3. Dwapar Yug (lasted 864,000 years)
4. Kali Yug (the current yug; started 5,000 years ago and will last for 432,000 years)

To give you some idea of the time frame of Indian cosmology, the Ramayana dates back to the Treta Yug and the Mahabharata to the Dwapar Yug. Our planet has existed for more than four billion years.

How does it feel to think of possibilities that many super intelligent, spiritually conscious beings could have lived, and possibly continue to live, among us in their astral or subtle bodies? Or that they may be on faraway planets, visiting us occasionally to speed up our evolution.?

Now if you ask me, 'Were the Puranas and Itihaas real?' or 'Did the Ramayana and Mahabharata really happen?' I may not have a definitive answer, but I want you to be open to possibilities and approach life with a curious mind, a clear heart, a welcoming attitude, and the willingness to learn, grow, transform and look at the bright side of life. Our attitudes towards life affect our behaviour and character. Our personalities are shaped by what we believe in our minds and hearts, leading us to our destinies.

Let us take the life of Lord Ganesha, the son of Lord Shiva. Lord Ganesha was guarding his mother's bathing area when his father became impatient and cut off his head. No caring father would do that. Even an impatient father wouldn't react to this extreme, least of all a father who is a role model for the entire universe. Through an extreme example, the story shows us how you should never resort to violence when angry. Even great people are bound to go through emotional bursts of anger or irrational behaviour; at that time, we may need to centre ourselves and act sensibly.

Lord Vishnu is the custodian of the universe in our Puranas. He is known to rest on the 'Ocean of Milk.' His wife, Goddess Lakshmi, sits on a pink lotus. The symbolic meaning of Lord Vishnu's state of rest is that his mind is at rest, clear of desires and ego.

The first teacher of the Heartfulness tradition, Pujya Lalaji Maharaj, explained to Pujya Babuji Maharaj, his disciple and the second teacher of Heartfulness, that Goddess Lakshmi (or the goddess of wealth) accompanies those who have subdued their numerous passions and egoism and keep them regulated. Does this mean that less desire gives more wealth? Just think about that!

Mother Saraswati, the goddess of knowledge, music, art and wisdom, is known to sit on a white lotus. But how can the lotus, which is so tiny, bear the weight of a woman? The intention is to convey the purity of learning, symbolised by the lotus, and the attitude of detachment (*vairagya*), like the lotus petal or leaf, which is unstained by muddy water. So that image befits a goddess of wisdom, doesn't it?

'Purusha Suktha', a hymn from the Rigveda, states that God has 1,000 different heads, 1,000 eyes, and 1,000 feet. Is this literal? No! The hyperbole means that God can see and know everything, be everywhere, and go anywhere. The universal being is omnipresent, omnipotent, omniscient, and even omnibenevolent. So the Puranas hold a deep symbolic significance and intrinsic wisdom.

Some parts of the stories from the Itihasas, such as the Ramayana and the Mahabharata, are interpolated and stretched. For example, Lord Hanuman was not a monkey commander (with a tail) of the monkey army; He was a great warrior with extraordinary capabilities and siddhis, who helped Lord Rama win the war against the ten-headed Ravana. Ravana had so much ego, the equivalent of ten heads, and at the same time, he is supposed to be very knowledgeable in the four Vedas and six Shastras. That's why his knowledge and ego are attributed to his ten heads.

While Dasaratha, as the name indicates, means ten raths, or chariots, does it mean he can ride ten chariots simultaneously? It actually means he has complete mastery of the ten senses—five outer senses and five inner senses.

Lord Krishna was not a romantic boyfriend for the Gopis or milkmaids, but one with wisdom and spiritual abilities. He was an icon of love, tenderness and devotion and also a spiritual teacher of his chief disciple Radha-ji and other Gopis. My spiritual guide, Babuji, spoke about the purely spiritual relationship between Lord Krishna as a boy and his associates. When Lord Krishna killed Kansa he was merely eleven years old. He left Vrindavan much before that. How would an eleven-year-old boy romance at such a young age? That too in a traditional orthodox society of those times? Radha-ji was older than Lord Krishna. She was married to someone quite older than Krishna.

Thus, stories are inherently attractive narratives and inspire us toward a good lifestyle. We need to emulate whatever inspires us and aspire to become better and reach our highest potential. When our enthusiasm is driven by a passion that springs from our deepest subconscious well, it fuels our imagination and opens us up to endless possibilities.

So go ahead. The stories are waiting for you! I shall meet you on the other side.

With love,
Daaji

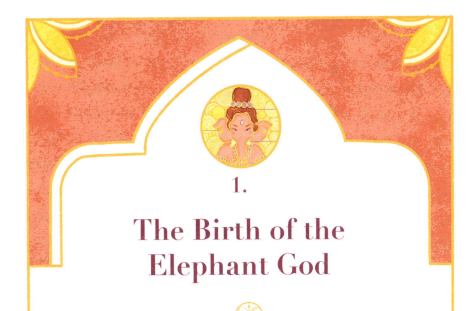

1.

The Birth of the Elephant God

Lord Ganesha's birthday is celebrated with great devotion, enthusiasm and fanfare. But how did Lord Ganesha come by to have the head of an elephant?

Once, when goddess Parvati, wife of Lord Shiva, was about to bathe, she asked Nandi, Shiva's bull, to guard her private bathing space. But when Lord Shiva came to the dwelling, Nandi was in a dilemma.

'Should I stop Lord Shiva from entering his own home?' Nandi wondered. 'I cannot disobey goddess Parvati, but how can I stop Lord Shiva?'

Finally, Nandi let Lord Shiva enter.

Parvati was upset with this. However, she understood that Nandi and the other *ganas*, or attendants, of Shiva were primarily his disciples and that they would prioritise him.

One day, not long after this incident, Parvati gathered the bathing mixture of sandalwood and dried turmeric from her own body and made a boy out of it. 'You are my son,' she said, infusing life into him. 'Go and guard my bathing chambers. No one should enter.'

The boy took goddess Parvati's words seriously. When Lord Shiva came home, the young boy did not let him through. 'Halt, sir!' he said. 'You may not enter. My mother is bathing.'

Unaware that the boy standing guard was his son, an enraged Shiva boomed, 'You impudent boy! How dare you stop me from entering my home?'

He raised his trident in a fury and cut the boy's head off.

Hearing the commotion, goddess Parvati quickly finished bathing and rushed out of her bathroom. On seeing her son lying dead, her anguish knew no bounds. It slowly turned into a blind rage. Lord Shiva was truly at a loss. If only he had known his wife had created the boy! Now Parvati's anger was threatening to destroy the whole universe.

'How can I placate Parvati?' Shiva wondered. Before Parvati could cause any damage, he called his ganas. 'Go and bring me the head of the first living being that you see,' he told them.

As the attendants searched the wilderness, the first living being they came across was a baby elephant. They cut its head and brought it to Lord Shiva. Using his spiritual powers, Lord Shiva placed the head on his son's body and brought him back to life.

To further appease Parvati, Shiva declared, 'I name my son Ganesha, the leader of my ganas.'

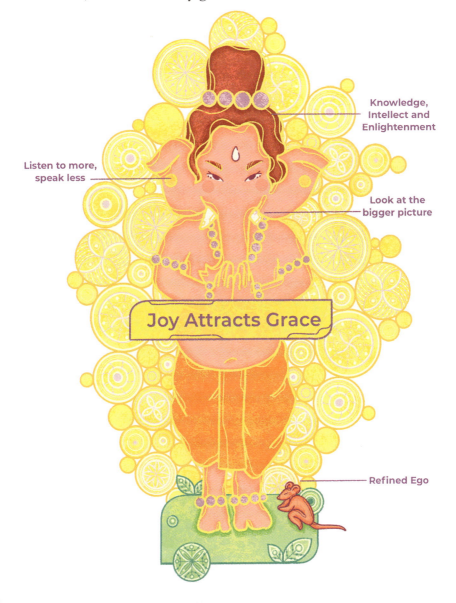

'Ganesha,' Shiva declared, 'will be the god of prosperous beginnings, and humanity will come to him to remove their obstacles.'

There are beautiful symbolisms associated with Lord Ganesha. His huge head stands for knowledge, intellect and enlightenment. His large ears and small mouth convey the message, 'Listen more; speak less.'

Lord Ganesha has only one tusk and there is a story behind that too. While writing the Mahabharata, one of the greatest epics in the world, his pen stopped working. As the contract with the author, Ved Vyas, was to write nonstop, Lord Ganesha broke off one of his tusks and continued writing with it.

Just like everything else associated with Lord Ganesha has a deeper meaning, so does his tiny and powerful vahan, or vehicle, the mouse. The great god transporting himself on the humble mouse is an indicator that we should be egoless and humble to such an extent that even a mouse can carry us effortlessly.

Do you get angry sometimes?

Have you been told anger is not a good thing to possess and that you must control it? Well, that's not entirely true. Anger, if appropriately addressed, can help us. However, when you find the emotion consuming you, you may want to take the following steps to direct it in a positive direction.

Release your anger

You can try the Left Nostril Breathing technique that activates the parasympathetic nervous system and calms you down. Your mind feels more relaxed.

Learn from your anger

If you approach anger with curiosity and caution, you will learn about your strengths and weaknesses. Be honest in your introspection and assess what you learn from anger. This will contribute to your self-improvement.

The Gift of Anger

Maintain a journal

Journalling is a great way to process your emotions. You could write down what made you angry. This could be anything: 'I did not get what I wished for', 'Someone said something', and so on. If you were to revisit your anger, think about what you would do differently.

2.

In Pursuit of Freedom

Sage Kashyap, one of the sapta rishis (seven wise Sages), had two wives—Kadru and Vinata. He decided to have children and so asked his wives, 'How many children do you want?'

'I want 1,000 brave sons,' Kadru said arrogantly, as she was asked first.

'I want just two sons, who are braver and and are also stronger than Kadru's,' Vinata said.

'May your wishes come true,' blessed Sage Kashyap.

Kadru became the mother of a thousand snakes. Among the prominent ones were Adhisesha (who is Lord Vishnu's seat) and Vasuki (the snake around Lord Shiva's neck).

Vinata gave 'birth' to two eggs that did not hatch for a long time. Losing patience, Vinata cracked open the first egg to find a child with beautiful wings and strong arms, but alas, no legs.

Vinata called him Aruna. He was angry with his mother for cracking the egg open before he could be fully formed.

He cursed his mother: 'May you be the slave of Kadru and her sons.'

In Pursuit of Freedom

Vinata was crestfallen. 'Son, I am sorry. What is the way to get out of this slavery?'

'Do not open the second egg,' Aruna said. 'Your second son will free you of slavery.' Aruna then flew away to become the charioteer of Surya, the sun god.

While Vinata waited for the second egg to hatch, Aruna's curse was coming true. Kadru tricked her into becoming a slave. One night, they both saw Uchchaihshravas, the white horse of Lord Indra.

'The tail of the horse is black,' Kadru said.

'No,' Vinata said, 'It's white.'

'Let us see it again in the morning,' Kadru said, 'If I am right, you must become my slave.' Vinata agreed as she knew the tail was white. To trick Vinata, Kadru told her sons, 'In the morning, go and sit on the tail of the horse so that it looks black.'

In the morning, Vinata and Kadru looked at the horse's tail. From afar it looked black. Vinata accepted defeat and became Kadru's slave. She knew she had been cheated.

Vinata waited patiently for her younger child to come into the world as he would liberate her from slavery. Finally, the egg hatched, and the mighty Garuda was born. He had the body of a human, the head of an eagle, mighty wings and the powers of a god. Like his mother, Garuda was also a slave to Kadru and her serpent sons. When his mother told him how she became a slave, Garuda became angry. 'Mother, you were enslaved through deceit,' he said.

'Yes, my son, but we must be patient. You will liberate us from this, as prophesied by your brother.'

One day, Garuda said to Kadru and her sons, 'Let us go free. We will give you whatever you ask in return.'

Kadru knew Garuda was powerful. So she wanted something worthwhile in the bargain. So she asked the impossible: 'Bring the nectar of immortality for my sons.'

Garuda agreed and set out on his adventure. He arrived at an island where he fed on the *nishadas* (fishermen tribe) and then flew to the mighty Himalayas to meet his father, Sage Kashyap. Garuda apprised his father of their current slavery situation and how Kadru sought nectar for their liberation.

Hearing this, Sage Kashyap said, 'A huge elephant and a massive tortoise have been fighting for years. Kill and eat them. Derive their strength, as you will need it for this mighty assignment.'

Garuda picked up the gigantic mammals in his talons and placed them on a tree branch. Just as he was about to eat them, the branch of the tree broke. At this moment, Garuda saw that along with the branch, the *valakhilya rishis*, or dwarf Sages, were also falling down. They are only as large as a thumb but highly intelligent with ascetic powers. Garuda saved them, and they blessed Garuda and told him that the nectar that he sought would be in Amaravati. Garuda then flew to Amaravati.

Meanwhile, Lord Indra was worried when he was informed about Garuda by his guru, Brihaspathi. He made preparations to protect the pot of nectar. Agni, the fire god, and Surya, the sun god, created a ring of fire around the pot. A thousand warriors stood guard. Indra created a giant rotating wheel with spikes. He laid the wheel flat and placed the pot on it. Two snakes stood guard just beside the pot. When the mighty Garuda came, he flapped his wings to send dust into the eyes of the warriors, but the wind god Vayu blew the dust away.

A focussed Garuda defeated Lord Indra, the *sadhyas* (demigods), the *gandharvas* (musicians), the aswin twins (physicians), the *vasus* (attendants), the *yakshas* (semigods) and many others. He sprouted multiple heads, filled his beak with water and sprayed it over the ring of fire guarding the pot of nectar. He killed the guards, broke the spokes of the wheel, killed the two serpents and picked up the pot of nectar.

An impressed Lord Vishnu, the protector and preserver of the universe, was watching all this. Garuda was so intent on freeing his mother that he did not even think of drinking a sip of the immortality nectar himself. Vishnu said, 'I give you the boon of immortality as you did not seek it for yourself. Also, I would like you to be my vehicle,' to which Garuda readily agreed.

Indra, who was observing this exchange, hurled his weapon vajra (made from the bones of Sage Dadhichi) at Garuda. The weapon struck Garuda who then said politely, 'Indra, king of devas, I respect you and honour Sage Dadhichi. So I shall shed a feather from my body even though the weapon did not harm me.'

After this incident, Garuda was called Suparna, one whose feathers are pretty.

Realising Garuda's greatness, Indra said, 'Forgive me and accept me as your friend.' Garuda accepted Indra's friendship.

Indra continued, 'I would also like to offer you a boon.' Garuda requested, 'Let the snakes be my food.'

'So be it,' said Indra, 'But do not give this pot of nectar to the snakes. If they become immortal, there will be chaos. They are poisonous. People need protection against them.'

'Then how will I free my mother?' Garuda asked.

'Give the snakes the pot and free your mother,' Indra said. 'Tell your half-brothers to drink from it only after bathing. By then I would have rescued the pot.' Again, Garuda agreed.

Garuda placed the pot of nectar on the kusa grass (a purifying grass born of the hair of Lord Vishnu) and said, 'This is from heaven and is the food of gods. So please first bathe yourselves, and only then you can touch the nectar.'

So, the snakes rushed to the river. As previously decided, Indra stealthily took the pot away. However, Indra dropped a few drops of the nectar on the grass. The snakes knew they'd been cheated so they rushed back to lick the fallen drops of nectar—only to have their tongues split by the sharp edges of the kusa grass. To this day their tongues remain split.

What is the secret of success?

What is that one quality that helps us succeed in life? Some people are successful because they are talented. But what really is the secret ingredient?

Revisit past successes

It would help if past successes are reviewed. How was success achieved at certain times and not others? Was it because of the effort made? Did the amount of effort put in differ? What happens when there is lack of interest? Would willpower help?

Create interest

Interest creates joy. Interest fuels resolve and gives the impetus to act. Why was Garuda successful? His only interest was to free his mother. It drove him to success. He envisioned only one goal and achieved it.

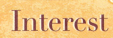

Interest

Choose wisely

Swami Vivekananda said, 'Take up one idea. Make that one idea your life—think of it, dream of it, live on that idea. Let the brain, muscles, nerves, every part of your body, be full of that idea and just leave every other idea alone. This is the way to success.'

Connect yourself within

We are all powered from an infinite source within: the divine. Take one step towards your success and the universe pushes you ten steps forward.

3.

One Fruit, Two Brothers

Lord Karthikeya, the god of war, is the younger brother of Lord Ganesha, and their parents were Lord Shiva and goddess Parvati. Once Sage Narada visited the family. 'I have brought a unique gift,' he told Lord Shiva and goddess Parvati, 'and I shall give it to only one of your children.'

'It is the fruit of wisdom,' said Narada. 'One who eats the fruit will acquire knowledge and wisdom.'

He continued, 'I have only one fruit and it cannot be shared. Lord Shiva can decide whom to give it to.'

Lord Shiva loved his children equally, so after consulting with his wife, he told his sons, 'Your mother and I have decided that both of you will take part in a challenge. You must circle the world once. Whoever finishes first can have the fruit of wisdom.'

Lord Karthikeya immediately mounted his vehicle, the beautiful and powerful peacock, and sped off to win the race. Goddess Parvati looked at her firstborn and said, 'Make haste, Ganesha. Go, run. This is a race.'

One Fruit, Two Brothers

Lord Ganesha knew that his vehicle, the humble slow-paced mouse, was nowhere near the peacock's speed. But Ganesha was not one to accept defeat.

After meditating for a while, Ganesha knew what he had to do. He went to his parents and with folded hands, he bowed before them and circled them. He bowed once again, then just stood there.

Everyone looked surprised.

'What is this strange act, dear?' Parvati asked.

With great humility, Ganesha replied, 'You created and breathed life into me. You and father are the world to me. So, I circled you and father.'

Lord Shiva was so pleased with Lord Ganesha's wit, simplicity and humility that

he declared him the winner. That is how Lord Ganesha got his fruit of wisdom.

My spiritual teacher Babuji Maharaj used to say, 'Be plain and simple to be identical with Nature.' That is a source of great wisdom. Ganesha's simplicity of thought and action led him to victory. Exploring creative solutions by thinking out of the box can solve complex problems.

How to find simple solutions to complex problems.

What does 'Think out of the box' mean? It means to approach a problem from a totally different perspective and find a solution that differs from the traditional way of thinking. But how is this done?

When you hit a wall, know the wall exists.

Sometimes, explaining the problem or predicament in detail solves it. Yes, admit that you hit a wall, and explain why and how that happened.

Do not break the wall. Go around it.

Don't try to look for the apparent solution that eludes you but look for alternatives. Broaden your perspective. Keep looking for other solutions till you find the best option.

Think Outside the Box

Look for invisible solutions

Many times, I have come across solutions for problems in the simplest of ways. Occasionally, the solutions come when I have a clear mind and pure heart. I go for long walks, or spend time with friends. When we are in a highly relaxed state, and in joy, we naturally find a way, just like the famous 'Eureka!' moment. Lord Ganesha found a solution in the same way when he sat down to meditate.

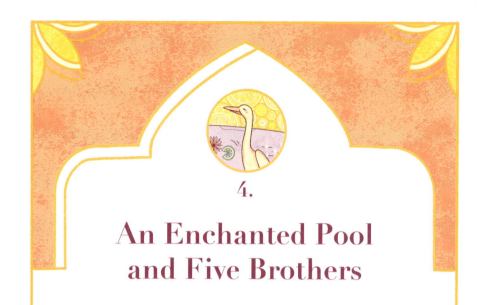

4.

An Enchanted Pool and Five Brothers

This is a story about the Pandavas—Yudhishthir, Bhima, Arjuna, Nakul and Sahadev.

While in exile in the forest, the Pandavas once discovered that a deer stole their firewood. They chased after the deer, who led them deeper into the woods. 'I am thirsty,' Yudhishthir said after a long chase.

'Let me climb a tree and see if there is a lake or pond nearby,' said Nakul.

'I see trees and shrubs that usually grow near water bodies,' Nakul said from atop a tree. 'Surely, there will be a pond in that direction.'

'Go, brother,' Yudhishthir said to Nakul. 'Fill your quiver with water and bring it back.'

As Nakul walked deeper into the forest, he came across a small stream that led to a pond filled with crystal-clear water. On the far edge of the pond stood a beautiful crane.

An Enchanted Pool and Five Brothers

As Nakul knelt to drink the water, the crane said, 'Do not drink this water until you answer my questions.'

Nakul was thirsty, so he ignored the voice, drank from the pool and fell dead instantly.

Meanwhile, Yudhishthir, having waited patiently for Nakul's return, asked Sahadev to look for their brother and bring some water too.

Sahadev found the pond and his brother, who lay dead on the ground. Sahadev was so thirsty that before doing anything else, he knelt to take a sip of the water when he heard the crane say sternly: 'Do not drink the water, Prince Sahadev. First, answer my questions.'

But he also did not heed the voice and drank the water. Soon Sahadev too lay dead.

Now Yudhishthir sent Arjuna, the greatest archer in the world. When Arjuna arrived at the pond, he also heard the same voice. Arjun shot a few arrows towards the crane, which had no effect on it. 'Come, fight with me,' he shouted, then drank the water but died within seconds.

Finally, Yudhishthir sent his only remaining brother, Bhima, who also met with the same fate. So Yudhishthir set off in the direction of the pond. As Yudhishthir reached the pool, he saw his dead brothers. He looked over the pond. It was pretty, with its water glittering like diamonds against the sun's rays, resplendent with pink lotus blossoms and one single crane at the far end of the pond.

'There are no human or animal footprints on the ground,' he thought. 'There is also no blood on the bodies of my brothers, their weapons are still intact. This must be the work of a spirit.'

As he knelt to drink the water, he heard the voice: 'Answer my questions before you drink the water.'

'Who are you, and what do you want?' asked Yudhishthir.

'I am a yaksha,' said the crane. Yakshas can be evil and sometimes they are worshipped as demigods.

'Oh yaksha, did you kill my brothers?' Yudhishthir asked.

'First answer my questions, or you will meet the same fate,' the yaksha said.

Yudhishthir agreed.

'Who makes the sun rise?' asked the yaksha.

'The Creator who made the universe,' Yudhishthir said.
'What is the highest duty of man?'
'Harm no one.'
'What is mightier than the earth and higher than the heavens?'
'The love of parents.'
'What is faster than the wind?'
'People's mind.'
'What makes people lovable?'
'When they are no longer proud.'
'What makes people happy?'
'When they have no desire, people acquire eternal happiness.'
'Who is the most difficult enemy to conquer?'
'Anger.'
'What is the most valuable possession?'
'Knowledge.'
'Who is the noblest of all humans?'
'Those who wish the well-being of all.'

And so it continued. It is said the yaksha asked Yudhishthir 126 questions. The prince answered each one wisely. Finally, the yaksha said, 'I am your spirit father, Yama-Dharma, the god of death. Disguised as a deer, I stole the firewood so that you would come searching for me. Now that you have answered all my questions, you may drink from the pond.'

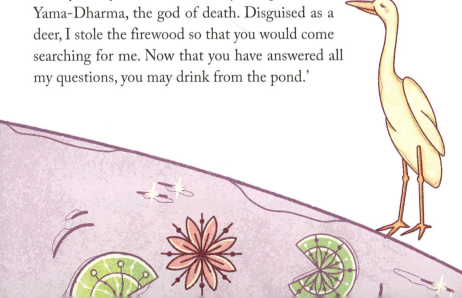

After Yudhishthir quenched his thirst, Yama said, 'I would like to give back the life of one of your brothers. Whom would you choose?'

'Please return Nakul to me,' Yudhishthir said.

'He is your half-brother,' Yama said. 'Why not one of your own brothers?'

'He is the son of Mother Madri, my father's younger wife. As the son of Kunti, the elder wife of my father, I am alive. It is only fair that Mother Madri also has a son who is alive.'

'You are not only fair and wise but are also impartial and noble. I return all your brothers to life.' Saying so, Lord Yama vanished, leaving Yudhishthir with his now alive and disoriented brothers.

How would one stay focussed during difficult moments? And act and say the right things at such times?

Listening to the heart is simple and easy. 'Follow your heart' is a common adage.

Challenging times call for focus

It is not easy to stay focussed during the most difficult moments (like the one Yudhishthira faced). But as in the story, it is possible.

Meditation can be good

Meditation is a simple act of self-introspection. A few minutes of silence and going deep into our hearts is all it takes.

Let the Heart Speak

Listening to the heart is rewarding

Listen to and follow your heart. It can be your inner guide. The heart speaks loudest when we listen to it. The more we listen, the more it guides us in the right direction.

Correct thinking, right understanding and honest approach to life

Your heart always knows the correct answer. How did Yudhishthira answer 126 questions correctly? He listened to his heart, thought with his mind and gave a clear explanation. This important trait of correct thinking leads to right understanding, which makes us take an honest approach to life.

5.

Jada Bharata's Journey

This story is about King Bharata who was the emperor of India. The country derives its ancient name of Bharata from this great ruler.

After his retirement from royal duties, King Bharata enjoyed a hermit life in the forest. He ate fruits from the trees, drank from a little stream and built a small hut in a clearing. All his time was spent in meditation. One day, he rescued an abandoned fawn whose mother had died immediately after giving birth.

The king tended to the baby deer and over time grew quite attached to the animal. As the deer grew up, it ventured into the forest to graze on its own but always returned home. At such times when the deer was away, Bharata worried about it. 'I hope a wild tiger or lion has not attacked my little baby.'

With time, the king grew old and weak. Even on his deathbed, instead of remembering god, King Bharata continued to worry about the deer. As a result, in his next birth, the king was born a deer. Now an evolved soul, wiser than before, Bharata remembered his previous life with regret. 'Alas,' he thought, 'it is my folly that at the time of death I did not spend time in meditation on the Lord, rather ruminated on the deer.'

King Bharata decided to compensate for abandoning his spiritual pursuit. So he grazed near ashrams and cottages of Sages who meditated, and kept remembering god in his heart.

As a result of his good karma as a deer, King Bharata was reborn as the youngest son of a Sage. In this current life also, he remembered his past two lives and was determined to avoid the attraction of worldly things. While still a child, Bharata stopped speaking and so everyone started calling him 'Jada Bharata', meaning 'mute' Bharata. He spent most of his time contemplating on god.

When the father died, the sons divided their property among themselves. Some of Jada Bharata's older brothers treated him unkindly because they thought he couldn't speak and thus

wouldn't tell on them. Moreover, he did not react to whatever they did. At times, when things became unbearable, he would take a walk to a nearby forest and sit there and meditate for some time under a tree, and when he felt better, he would go back home.

He was determined to realise god in this birth.

Once, while Bharata was resting under a tree, King Rahugana, the ruler of that country, passed by in a palanquin. One of his servants carrying the palanquin fell ill, so Jada Bharata was requested to take his place.

While carrying the palanquin, Jada Bharata made sure not to step on ants and other insects on the ground. As a result of this, the palanquin kept rocking from side to side, making the king's ride bumpy and uncomfortable. 'You fool!' the king said, 'Are you so weak that you cannot carry this palanquin properly? Do you need some rest?'

'Who did you call a fool?' Jada Bharata asked.

The king was surprised to hear a response.

'Do you mean this body is a fool?' Jada Bharata asked. 'Our bodies are composed of the same thing—flesh, blood and bones.'

'Do you call this mind a fool?' he continued. 'Our minds are the same. Everyone has the same mind with the same faculties.'

'Or, by "you", do you mean the Higher Self inside us? That also is the same for everyone.

'I do not need rest. I was avoiding stepping on the creatures on the ground.'

The king realised that this young boy was more than a mere fool. He could sense the wisdom of the boy's words and stepped down from the palanquin.

'Forgive me, Oh, wise one!' the king said. 'I did not realise who you were. Teach me more. I was looking for a guru and you are here.'

'The Higher Self inside us can never become exhausted,' Jada Bharata said. 'The Higher Self is the ultimate source, or the essence of everything in the universe, and it is omnipotent and omnipresent.' They sat down and spoke about the secrets and mysticism of the soul. Jada Bharata also shared a secret that god realisation is attained neither through chanting nor austerity but only through one who has already attained Realisation. Jada Bharata introduced the king to meditation and to the god within the heart.

After the king parted company, Jada Bharata continued with his spiritual journey and was freed from the cycle of birth and death.

What is the point of life and death?

We are all born and one day, we must all die. What do we do in in our journey of life and death?

What do we do every day?

Besides our daily routine, we indulge in hobbies. We learn in school, from friends and from elders. We spend time in activities that keep us mentally and physically fit. In doing so, we seek happiness and meaning to life.

What motivates us?

At times we like to do certain things and not others. The next day that changes. Some of us may like to learn to dance or sing or learn new languages or study computer coding. There are certain things we are drawn to more than others. Those are things we are passionate about and destined to do.

A Higher Purpose to Existence

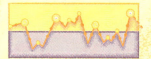

Growth mindset

Sometimes we falter despite knowing what we need to do. It is okay. We must pick ourselves up, move on and find alternate ways to reach our goal. Our abilities have the potential to improve through our efforts. When we understand this process of growth, we are motivated from within.

Enriching life qualities

We grow and evolve by refining our qualities and attitudes. Our hobbies, friends, life decisions and so on, all assist us. Heartfulness Meditation helps develop qualities like love, acceptance, humility, service, compassion and empathy, and helps us attain a higher purpose in life.

6.

Hanuman Shows Humility

Lord Hanuman is known for his devotion to Lord Rama. He is also known for his valour, strength and courage, but above all, for his humility.

Ramayana is full of instances where Lord Hanuman's humility is revealed. One such instance is when Hanuman went to Lanka in search of Mother Sita, Lord Rama's wife.

When he was flying over the sea, Hanuman came across a huge mountain called Mainaka who asked him to rest.

Hanuman said, 'Thank you, but I have to go. Every minute is precious. Lord Rama awaits news of his beloved wife.'

The other gods also wanted to test Hanuman's prowess and intelligence in fulfilling such an arduous mission. They asked Surasa, the mother of snake gods: 'Mother Surasa, could you confirm if Hanuman is capable of this mighty task?'

Surasa agreed and while Hanuman was flying over the ocean, she appeared before him disguising herself as a fearful monster.

'You are my food for today,' she said loudly, 'Fly into my mouth so that I can gobble you up.'

'I am on an important mission. Kindly permit me to go,' Hanuman requested.

'I cannot let you go. According to a boon from Lord Brahma, if anyone is flying past this area and wants to go further, that person has to pass through my mouth,' she replied.

'I shall return this way,' Hanuman reasoned, 'and you can eat me then.' But Surasa did not relent.

Hanuman finally consented and said, 'On one condition, I shall enter your mouth. It should grow as large as I can grow.' Surasa agreed to this. So now Hanuman assumed a gigantic form, almost to a 100 yojanas (an ancient measure equivalent to about eight miles). Surasa also grew bigger and made her mouth large enough to accommodate Lord Hanuman's immense form. This continued on and on, till they both grew huge.

Just as Surasa was about to eat Hanuman, he shrunk himself to the size of a thumb and flew in and out of her mouth in a jiffy. Hanuman then said, 'Now I have fulfilled your condition. I have entered your mouth and come out of it. So, please let me go now.'

Surasa admired Hanuman's intellect, ingenuity and courage, and was pleased with him. She assumed her true form of a pretty lady.

'I bless you, my son,' she said. 'Go and find Mother Sita. I was merely testing your strength and wisdom.'

Off then, Hanuman flew to Lanka.

Does this story remind you of Antman, the Marvel superhero who could become big and small at will? He destroys evil. Then there's the story of David and Goliath in the Bible. David as a small boy is not afraid of the huge and fierce Goliath. His strength and courage come from god.

Strength and intellect are not defined by size. Wisdom comes through humility and Hanuman is a role model for this.

How does one develop humility?

We often think humility is a sign of weakness. In reality, humility is the mother of all virtues. But let us know more about it.

What is humility?

Humility is flexibility. It does not mean to let go, but to use our strengths to the best of our advantage. We often win arguments but lose relationships if we are not humble. A wise person knows that ego is for self-improvement and not for ascertaining supremacy.

Does humility mean lack of confidence?

Humility does not mean being shy or lack of confidence. Lord Hanuman was both regal and humble simultaneously.

Flexibility

Humility, flexibility and simplicity

Hanuman realised that by becoming bigger, he could not win, but by becoming very tiny, he could succeed. Have you noticed that during discussions or arguments, when things come to a heated place, and when suddenly you let the other person have their way, you have a sense of fulfilment, success and peace?

7.

An Unnatural Heaven

King Trishanku from the Ikshvaku dynasty was a noble and upright king. But he had an unnatural wish—he wanted to go to heaven while he was still alive.

To fulfil his wish, he approached Sage Vasishta. But Sage Vasishta refused, 'Nobody can ascend heaven in their physical body,' he said. 'You should remove such unnatural thoughts from your mind.'

Trishanku was not willing to take no for an answer. So, he asked Vasishta's sons for help. They too refused and this angered Trishanku. So, he insulted them and in response the sons of Vasishta cursed Trishanku, 'May you stink like a corpse for a long time.'

Trishanku then approached Guru Vishwamitra, who agreed to help him after learning that Sage Vasishta had refused.

When Vishwamitra started the rituals for Trishanku to ascend heaven in his bodily form, the gods disapproved of it, as it was against Nature. 'We do not accept the offerings from the holy fire of Trishanku's ritual,' they said. 'And we do not grant permission for Trishanku to enter heaven'.

Angry with the gods, Vishwamitra vowed to send Trishanku to heaven using his yogic powers. As Trishanku began to ascend towards heaven by Vishwamitra's powers, Lord Indra pushed him down towards the earth. However, Vishwamitra stopped Trishanku's descent and created another heaven in the middle of the skies for him.

When Vishwamitra was about to create one more Indra to rule that second heaven, Lord Indra and Lord Brahma stopped him. They said, 'Don't you know that no one in their physical body can enter heaven? Do not disrupt the natural laws of this universe.'

Vishwamitra could see the wisdom in Brahma's words; however, he was also bound by his promise to Trishanku. Eventually, as a compromise, the gods permitted Trishanku to stay in the second heaven created by Vishwamitra as it lay midway between earth and heaven. So now Trishanku was 'stuck' there.

In India, there is a saying, 'hanging like Trishanku', meaning in a state of limbo, to be neither 'here' nor 'there'. This 'hanging' happened because of Vishwamitra's ego and Trishanku's unnatural desire.

Trishanku is today known as the Southern Cross constellation and is visible in the Southern skies.

What is a natural thing to wish and pray for?

Traditionally, we understand prayer as an act of asking for something from God. But prayer is not merely an esoteric, it is a tool for self-improvement too.

Purpose of a prayer

Prayer is an intention. It is also a call for help and guidance. It creates a connection with the core of our hearts. We may call it divine or attribute it to a superconscious state from where we receive guidance or wisdom.

What do we seek through prayer?

We seek to remove unwanted behaviours, and worries that bring suffering. When such a prayer is a cry of feeling from one's heart, it is easily heard. Through prayer we seek continuous improvement, acquire noble qualities, grow and evolve. It leads to rightness in action and perfection in character.

Rightness in Action and Perfection in Character

A special prayer

Every night before going to bed, one must reflect on the day and pray. Repeat the words of the Heartfulness prayer. Understand the words and observe the feelings that these words evoke. Become one with those feelings and close your eyes in sleep by becoming the feeling that the prayer creates.

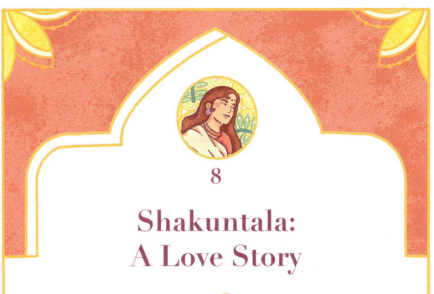

8

Shakuntala: A Love Story

Our story begins when Sage Kanva found two newborn babies in the forest. In the absence of their parents, the babies were being guarded by the Shakunta birds. So, Sage Kanva named the girl Shakuntala and the boy Pramati.

Shakuntala was the daughter of Sage Vishwamitra and Menaka. Like her mother, Shakuntala was extremely beautiful. Sage Vishwamitra wanted to pursue a spiritual life and Menaka wanted to return to the heavens and continue as a celestial dancer. Thus, Shakuntala grew up in Sage Kanva's care.

While chasing a deer on a hunting trip, King Dushyanta happened to see Shakuntala, who was by now a young maiden, and was smitten by her beauty. Shakuntala was also drawn towards the handsome King Dushyanta. So, when he proposed marriage, Shakuntala consented. Theirs was a *gandharva vivah* or a marriage between consenting adults with no ceremony or ritual and no witnesses.

Before returning to his palace, Dushyanta gave Shakuntala his royal ring and said, 'This will remind you of me until I come back.'

A lovelorn Shakuntala spent most of her time daydreaming about Dushyanta. It was during one such time that the hermitage was visited by Sage Duruvasa, who was known for being short-tempered. When he wasn't venerated by Shakuntala, the irritable Sage felt ignored and insulted. In anger, Duruvasa cursed Shakuntala: 'May the person you are thinking about forget you'.

Shakuntala's friend, who was with her at that time, pleaded with Duruvasa. 'Please do not misunderstand

Shakuntala,' she said. 'She is newly married and misses her husband.'

Duruvasa took pity on Shakuntala and relented, 'Your husband will remember you when he sees a gift he gave you,' he said.

As time passed, in Dushyanta's absence, Shakuntala gave birth to a baby boy whom she called Bharata. This child would eventually grow up to become one of the greatest rulers of India, who would unify the country and call it Bharata after himself.

Shakuntala wanted father and son to meet, so she decided to go to her husband. While travelling on a boat, Shakuntala lost her ring when she dipped her hands in the water. The ring was swallowed by a fish.

When Shakuntala came to Dushyanta's court, nobody recognised her—not even the king. Dushyanta asked her, 'Who are you and how can I help you?'

'I am your wife,' she said. 'Don't you remember me?'

The king was surprised. 'No, I have never seen you before,' he said.

Shakuntala immediately realised this was due to Sage Duruvasa's curse. Since she had lost the ring the king had given her, she had no means of proving who she was. So, humiliated and distraught, Shakuntala returned home.

With time, Bharata grew up to be a fine young boy at the ashram of Sage Kanva. He was brave and often played with lions and tigers, among other animals.

Far away in another part of the kingdom, a fisherman cut open the fish that had swallowed Shakuntala's ring. He thought of the royal reward he could get upon returning the ring to the king. So, he immediately went to the palace.

When the king saw the ring, he instantly remembered Shakuntala and their secret marriage and that she had come to visit him. Duruvasa's curse was lifted, and Dushyanta went looking for his wife and son.

In the forest he found a little boy who was counting the teeth of a lion. Dushyanta was impressed with the boy's bravery and asked him, 'Who are you and where are your parents?'

'I am Prince Bharata,' said the young boy innocently, 'the son of King Dushyanta and Shakuntala.'

A happily shocked King Dushyanta asked his son to take him to his mother. After a happy reunion, Dushyanta brought his family to the palace.

What is true love?

The story of Shakuntala and Dushyanta is a journey of love. But have you wondered what it means to be in true love?

Transcending the expectation of love

Seek the fulfilment of love within your heart, rather than in an external expression. In love, there is no place for expectation. Only for gratitude. That is why love is the pinnacle of human nobility.

True love

In true love, only love exists, with the lover and beloved dissolved in it. Here there is no giving and taking of love. They both become love. My guru, Babuji Maharaj, used to say, 'Love is the inner awakening to reality.' That is a very subtle experience.

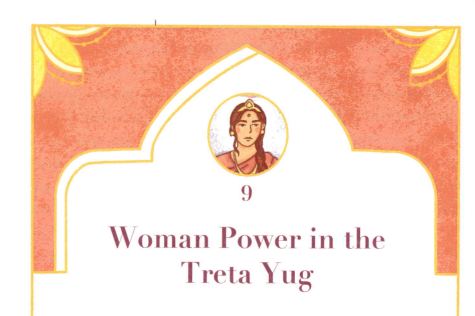

9

Woman Power in the Treta Yug

Within the Ramayana lies another story—that of the death of Sahasra Ravana at the hands of Sita. Sage Valmiki who wrote the Ramayana narrated this story to another Sage, Bharadwaj.

Rama and Sita were warmly welcomed back to Ayodhya after their victory in Lanka. Everyone was singing praises of Rama's victory over the ten-headed Ravana.

Sita was much amused and was smiling all the time. A courtier asked, 'Mother Sita, why are you smiling ?'

'Winning against the ten-headed Ravana is a courageous act,' she said. 'But do you know how we defeated Sahasra Ravana, the thousand-headed Ravana?'

Sita narrated that story to the court.

After Ravana's death, his thousand-headed demon brother, Sahasra Ravana, started wreaking havoc on the world. This compelled Lord Rama to start a battle with him.

Sahasra Ravana had 1,000 heads and 2,000 arms and lived on a distant island called Pushkara. He was said to be more powerful than the ten-headed Ravana, but unlike him, he did not have a boon from Lord Brahma.

Lord Rama and the armies of Sugreeva and Vibhishana waged a battle against Sahasra Ravana's army. Sahasra Ravana used vayu-astra, the weapon given to him by the wind god, and blew Lord Rama's army out of Pushkara. Angered by this, Lord Rama used the lethal brahma-astra, given to him by Sage Agastya.

However, Sahasra Ravana caught the arrow and broke it in two. Lord Rama was unnerved by this. In that one moment of weakness, Sahasra Ravana shot an arrow that rendered Lord Rama unconscious. This led to panic.

Just then a loud, strong and angry laugh came from the battlefield. Everyone turned and saw Mother Sita who had taken the form of the grand destroyer goddess, Kali. She looked terrifying. Sita took a sword and cut off the 1,000 heads of Sahasra Ravana in one stroke. Innumerable divine mothers came out of Mother Kali and started destroying the demon army.

Seeing the destruction, the gods grew worried and appealed for her to stop.

'My husband looks like he is dead,' she said. 'If you can revive him then I shall relent.'

So Lord Brahma restored Lord Rama to life. After he regained consciousness and saw Mother Sita, he became worried.

'Do not worry, Rama,' Lord Brahma assured him. 'Now that you are alive, Mother Sita will come back to her human form. She took this form to defeat your slayer, the Sahasra Ravana. Without Shakti, our mother, the Lord's task of creation and destruction cannot be accomplished.'

Sita let Rama see her divine celestial vision, or Darshan. Later, they all returned to Ayodhya, and narrated this incident to many others.

This story shows how Lord Rama's companion and wife, Mother Sita, is also his protector. This story is described in Adhbut Ramayana or Wonderful Ramayana.

What is woman power?

We've known Sita as compassionate, loving and devoted to Rama. Did you know she was a warrior too?

Independent thinking and womanhood

Women have been associated with independent thought and action, of valour and courage. History has known women to have changed the course of civilisations through their courageous actions.

Significance of femininity

Did you know, Sage Gritsamada prayed for a daughter even though he had a hundred sons? In ancient times, femininity was not only important but was also considered holy.

Courage of the Heart

Man and woman are one

According to the ancient philosophy of India, man and woman—Shiva and Shakthi—are one. Their importance is equal in this universe. They complement each other and make up for each other's weaknesses. In Adhbut Ramayan, Mother Sita rose to the occasion. She defeated the mighty asura and brought Lord Rama back to life.

10

Bhagiratha: An Adventure in Perseverance

In ancient times, kings established supremacy by conducting Ashwamedha yagna, a horse sacrifice ritual.

In this sacrifice, a horse, accompanied by the king's finest warriors, was let loose on a journey around the kingdoms for a whole year. It ended once the horse returned to the yagna after roaming unchallenged and redrawing the kingdom's boundaries. The return of the horse indicated the completion of the ceremony.

One such king who undertook an Ashwamedha yagna was King Sagara of Ayodhya. However, Lord Indra felt insecure and

worried that King Sagara was perhaps competing for his heavenly position. So, he abducted the horse and tied it in the hermitage of Sage Kapil. King Sagara sent out his 60,000 sons in search of the horse. When they found the horse, they wrongly assumed that the Sage had stolen it. They rudely roused up the Sage from his deep meditation. Angered with their accusation, Sage Kapil burnt all 60,000 sons of King Sagara down to ashes with the power gained from his penance.

When his sons did not return, King

Sagara sent his grandson, Amshuman, who found the ashes of his father and uncles at Sage Kapil's ashram.

When Amshuman tried to conduct the last rites of his family members, Lord Garuda, the king of birds, interrupted him. 'Your father and uncles have been cursed and burnt by Sage Kapil. Their souls could reach heaven only by immersing their ashes in the holy waters of River Ganga.'

'That will take a long time,' Garuda said, advising, 'It is better to go back with the horse and complete the yagna.'

Over the years, King Sagara and his descendants tried to bring the holy river Ganga to earth but were unsuccessful. One such descendant was King Bhagiratha.

On his deathbed, King Dileepa told his son, 'My dear Bhagiratha, when you ascend the throne, your first duty is to bring the river Ganga from the heavens and liberate your ancestors.'

Bhagiratha consulted his teachers and guides. They all said, 'Son! Meditate and pray to achieve this.'

Bhagiratha handed over his kingdom's administrative responsibilities to his ministers and went into the forest to pray to Lord Brahma. After years of penance, Lord Brahma granted Bhagiratha a boon of his choice. Bhagiratha asked for River Ganga to come down to Earth.

'Earth would not be able to sustain the rapid and powerful flow of River Ganga,' Lord Brahma said.

'Only Lord Shiva can withstand the forceful fall of River Ganga onto Earth,' said Lord Brahma, 'and if he agrees to do it, then I shall request Mother Ganga to come down to Earth.'

Bhagiratha's next task was to seek Lord Shiva's help. Bhagiratha ate no food, drank no water, but living on air alone, he prayed to please Lord Shiva. The compassionate Lord was pleased with Bhagiratha's penance and agreed.

In heaven, Ganga was admired, appreciated and much revered. As a result, she had become vain and did not like being told what to do. Since she could not refuse Lord Brahma's orders, she roared down to Earth with her full force. Everyone was terrified by her powerful flow and worried for Mother Earth. However, just at the right moment, Lord Shiva caught the falling river's wild cascade in his matted hair.

Ganga struggled to free herself, but Shiva would not release her as he was unhappy with her arrogance. Lord Shiva eventually

relented when Bhagiratha requested that he let the Ganga flow uninterrupted.

It is said that Bhagiratha, riding his mighty chariot, led the way for the holy river Ganga. On the way Sage Jahnu was disturbed by the mighty flow and roaring noise of the River Ganga and, in anger, he swallowed the river completely. It is only after Bhagiratha pleaded that he needed River Ganga to liberate his ancestors that Sage Jahnu let out the impish river through his ears. Thus, Ganga is also called Jahnavi in some parts of India, which means the 'daughter of Sage Jahnu'.

When Ganga flowed over the ashes of Bhagiratha's ancestors, King Sagar's 60,000 sons were instantly liberated.

Pleased with Bhagiratha's perseverance, Lord Brahma declared his effort as Bhagiratha-prayatna, which is now an Indian metaphor for 'supreme effort'. Even today, millions of Indians believe that after the cremation of their departed elders, immersing their ashes in river Ganga helps liberate their souls.

How can we succeed in life?

Taking shortcuts has a great appeal, but there is no real shortcut to ultimate success. Here are some tips to succeed in life.

Define your goals

Bhagiratha's goals were clear to him and that clarity contributed to his success. What are your short- and long-term goals? Write down your goals and ways of achieving them. This can help gain focus and clarity.

Persist. Persevere. Prevail

Bhagiratha faced many obstacles, but persevered and prevailed over each hurdle until he succeeded. It may take more than one attempt to reach a goal, but one must keep trying till they succeed.

Perseverance

Anything is possible. Believe it!

It is natural to move to greener pastures at first sight of an obstacle. Bringing down the river Ganga from heaven to earth seemed unattainable. Yet it was done. Expand your possibilities and your goals. What the mind can conceive can be achieved. You just need to find a way.

Be joyful

Work on your goals and succeed. However, life is a journey of joy. So, lighten up and smile a little, along the way. My spiritual teacher, Babuji Maharaj, used to say, 'Joy attracts grace.' And without the grace of god, is anything ever possible? Did you just now wonder if Bhagiratha was joyful? The short answer is, 'Yes!' If not for the grace of god, he wouldn't have succeeded.

11

An Epitome of Faith and Confidence

Long ago, there lived a wise Sage called Mrikandu. He and his wife, Marudhvathi, were devotees of Lord Shiva. However, they were sad because they had no children. So they prayed to Lord Shiva, and pleased with their devotion and sincerity, Lord Shiva granted them the boon of a child. But alas, there is a twist in this tale.

Lord Shiva gave Mrikandu a choice. 'Do you want a son who is pious, wise and virtuous, but lives for only 16 years? Or do you want a son who may be evil and dim-witted, but will have a long life?'

Without hesitating Mrikandu said, 'We would like to have a son who is worthy of your blessings, even if his life is short.'

Lord Shiva smiled and granted Mrikandu his wish. Soon after, Marudhvathi gave birth to a son and the couple called him Markandeya.

By the time Markandeya was five years old, he had already mastered the Vedas, the Shastras and the Sutras. When

Markandeya was eight years old, Mrikandu said to his wife, 'It is time to perform the Upanayanam for our son.' Upanayanam is a ritual that marks the end of childhood and the initiation into spiritual knowledge. So Markandeya learnt the Gayatri Mantra, one of the oldest and most powerful Sanskrit mantras that inspires wisdom and enlightenment.

Very soon, Markandeya celebrated his fifteenth birthday. Instead of being happy, Markandeya's parents were sad. They remembered Lord Shiva's boon and knew in a year's time their son would die. Markandeya sensed their sorrow. 'Mother, and Father,' he said, 'Why are you so sad?' On Markandeya's repeated prodding, his parents told him about the boon. 'I do not know how to save you from your imminent death,' said his father.

'Please do not worry,' Markandeya said calmly, 'I am grateful to be born to noble parents such as you both. Now that I know about your boon from Lord Shiva, I can spend the rest of my days in the remembrance of god.'

'Bless me, Father,' he continued. 'I want to pray to Lord Shiva for wisdom and the way forward.' Mrikandu blessed his son and said, 'May you win over death.'

Markandeya meditated in a Shiva temple for nearly a year. Aware of Lord Shiva's boon to Mrikandu, the Lord of Death, Yama, sent his assistants to take the teenager's life. However, the assistants soon returned empty-handed. 'Lord,' they said, 'the radiance from this young boy is so powerful that we cannot approach him.'

'Let me visit him,' Lord Yama said and set out on his black buffalo, carrying a rope with a noose on one end to pull the soul from Markandeya's body.

As he approached the boy, Lord Yama wondered, 'I cannot let him live even a minute longer, but should I do so as he is meditating?'

'Let me do my duty,' Yama finally decided and threw the rope but the noose got caught in Markandeya's neck as well as the Shivalinga.

So, when Yama yanked the rope, the Shivalinga broke free. Enraged at his disciple being disturbed while praying, an angry Shiva came out of the Shivalinga that was in front of Markandeya and killed Yama.

When the other gods saw Lord Yama dead, they became worried. What would happen to all the creatures on the planet, they wondered. The gods then pleaded with Lord Shiva, 'Please restore the life of the god of death. Without him, there will be chaos.' Shiva relented and Lord Yama came back to life. Pleased with Markandeya's devotion, Shiva blessed him with immortality. 'Death can never touch you. You will always be sixteen and never grow old.'

Thus, Markandeya became one of the chiranjeevis, or the immortals who would live until the end of Kali Yuga, according to the scriptures.

How can we achieve the apparently impossible?

In the story of Bhagiratha, we saw the importance of perseverance which is very important for success. Even greater than that kind of tenacity and purposefulness, the quality of confidence is important. How to become confident?

Silence your inner critic

Markandeya knew he could win over death. That kind of confidence comes when our faith is strong. So there is no question of silencing the inner critic. The inner voice guides and we follow.

Faith and Confidence

Practice cheerful acceptance

Suppose the task we embark on leads to failure, how do we move on? We accept the situation. We are all human, we make mistakes and learn from them. There is nothing wrong with failure. Suppose if Markandeya would have died, he still would have lived a lovely young life and would have been honoured along with the gods for his virtue and piety, wouldn't he?

The idea of faith

What is faith? My spiritual teacher, Pujya Babuji Maharaj, said 'Faith is a lively link connecting the mortal with the immortal.' We don't know the immortal god. To experience sense of immortality in our hearts takes time. Faith comes from believing that it may be possible god exists, and asking to experience him.

12

Moving on from Mistakes

Kaka Bhushundi is an immortal crow Sage who was a devotee of Lord Shiva. He was born in Ayodhya, the birthplace of Lord Rama, but he disliked Rama and spoke rudely about him, in spite of having a teacher who tried to instil in him a love for Lord Rama.

Kaka Bhushundi saw Lord Rama as a mere mortal and inferior to Lord Shiva. This eventually irked Lord Shiva who cursed Kaka Bhushundi to be born as a serpent. Kaka Bhushundi's teacher became sad by this and requested Lord Shiva to forgive his disciple.

Lord Shiva relented. 'I cannot withdraw my curse. But Kaka Bhushundi will incarnate a thousand times, in births that are lower than the human form. He will remember every birth and will progress spiritually and eventually become a devotee of Lord Rama.'

The cycle of birth and death continued for Kaka Bhushundi for a thousand births. Since Shiva had blessed him with love for

Lord Rama, he was born into a Sage's family and learnt to love Lord Rama.

As he grew older, Kaka Bhushundi went on pilgrimages and learnt more about Lord Rama. Here he met Sage Lomasa, a renowned scholar. 'How do I meditate on Lord Rama's physical form?' he asked the Sage. Kaka Bhushundi was attached to the form of god. Lomasa taught him that form is perishable, even the form of a divine person or an avatar like Lord Rama or Lord Krishna. He tried to teach Kaka Bhushundi about love and devotion to the formless aspect of god. While Lomasa taught many aspects of spirituality, Kaka Bhushundi merely focused on Lord Rama. This irked Sage Lomasa who cursed Kaka Bhushundi: 'You are not paying attention to my pearls of wisdom. You are focusing on only one aspect. I curse you to be transformed into a crow.'

Kaka Bhushundi accepted this. 'I merely wish to remember Lord Rama. It does not matter whether I am a crow or a human.' He was then transformed into a crow and flew away.

Later, Sage Lomasa regretted his curse and called Kaka Bhushundi back, recited the entire *Ramacharitamanas* and gave him a boon: 'May your devotion for Lord Rama be evergreen.' The boon was echoed from the heavens above.

An elated Kaka Bhushundi took leave of Sage Lomasa and retired to his ashram where he lived as a crow for all the kalpas (a period of 4.32 billion years in Vedic calendar, wherein the whole creation is dissolved and recreated after each kalpa) of creation.

It is said that Kaka Bhushundi resides outside of time, that he can witness every creation and destruction of the universe. He has witnessed the events mentioned in the Ramayana and the Mahabharata. In every new cycle of creation, when Lord Rama is born, Kaka Bhushundi flies to Ayodhya to admire his childhood.

Once upon a time, while fighting in Lanka, Rama and his brother Lakshmana fell unconscious because of the snake-powered arrows of Ravana's son Indrajeet. The two lay unconscious, bound by snakes that gripped them tightly while releasing venom that was getting absorbed in their bodies.

Fearing the worst, the gods arranged for Garuda, the king of birds with a face of an eagle and the body of a man, to rescue the brothers. Knowing Garuda would eat them, the snakes slithered away in fear. Slowly, Rama and Lakshmana regained consciousness.

When Lord Rama thanked Garuda for saving his life, Garuda felt confused about Lord Rama's divinity. 'Lord Rama is my Master as he is Lord Vishnu's avatar. Vishnu, or Rama in this incarnation, is here to save the world. But if I had not saved him today, he would have died. How can I now depend on him as my god? He is just an ordinary mortal who could not even destroy a few venomous snakes.'

When Garuda's doubt troubled him more, he shared it with Sage Narada, the author of the *Bhakti Sutras* that celebrate the relationship between god and devotees. Sage Narada suggested that Garuda ask Lord Shiva. But Lord Shiva directed Garuda to the ancient Kaka Bhushundi who was living in his own ashram in

the Himalayas. Narada asked Shiva, 'Why did you send Garuda to Kaka Bhushundi? You could have cleared his doubt yourself.'

Shiva replied, 'His ego clouds his understanding. He thinks that as the king of birds, he is all powerful. Only by visiting Kaka Bhushundi who has the form of a humble crow can Garuda learn wisdom. His ego will dissove, and humility will grow in his heart.'

The crow Sage chastised Garuda for doubting the Almighty: 'Lord Rama merely gave you an opportunity to serve him. He is the incarnation of Lord Vishnu. You are a fool to doubt him and his love for you. Out of his love and concern for your evolution and growth, he gave you an opportunity to serve Him in this capacity.'

Garuda now understood things clearly. He then asked several questions on spirituality and Kaka Bhushundi answered all of Garuda's questions patiently. Some of them are here:

'Which is the highest form?' Garuda asked.

'The human form is the highest form. It is from this form that the soul attains god realisation and liberation,' Kaka Bhushundi replied.

'What is the greatest pain?' Garuda asked next.

'Poverty of love, wisdom and resources,' Kaka Bhushandi replied.

'What is the most joyous thing in this universe?'

'The company and blessing of saints.'

'What is the pinnacle of human excellence?'

'According to the Vedas, compassion for all living beings is the pinnacle of human excellence.'

'What is the worst sin?'

'Ingratitude is the worst sin. Do not be ungrateful to parents, your guru, god and saints. They are the people who bring grace to this world.'

'Does the mind have diseases?'

'Lust, greed and anger are the worst diseases. They cause derangement of the mind.'

After spending time with Kaka Bhushundi, all the doubts that Garuda had vanished. He returned to serve his master Lord Vishnu with humility and devotion.

How can we realise our mistakes and move forward?

> As human beings, we may make mistakes. But how do we discern and rectify these errors?

Mistakes are superficial

Nobody can commit an unforgivable sin. There is always a remedial part. I remember a couplet that my spiritual teacher talked about.
'*Gunegaro ko dekha jo unki rehmat ne,
bahut khafif hue jo gunegar na the.*'
It means that when god's merciful eyes fell upon sinners, even the virtuous were astounded by the gifts that the sinners received from god. Should we also become sinners to attract the grace of the lord? No. We must keep this idea that, 'Oh Lord, I made a mistake. I am sorry. Please forgive me and make me deserving of your grace.'

Allow for transformation

When transformation happens within yourself, accept it. Let go of prejudices and allow yourself to grow. In Kaka Bhushundi and Garuda's story, there were instances of arrogance and subsequent wisdom. Kaka Bhushundi's transformation from someone who hated Lord Rama to becoming one of his greatest devotees is amazing. Similarly, Garuda got rebuked by a mere crow, and in doing so, gained spiritual enlightenment. This is a humbling but rewarding experience. Garuda also allowed his doubts about Lord Rama to be washed away. A heartfelt call for help and support is all that is required at such moments of doubt, ignorance and faltering.

13

Churning the Ocean of Milk

Once upon a time, when Lord Indra, the king of devas, was returning home to Indralok on his white elephant he met Sage Durvasa. Durvasa offered him a special garland that symbolised fortune. Though Indra placed the garland on his elephant's trunk, the smell of the flowers irritated the animal, and it threw the garland on the floor.

This irked the Sage who was known for his temper. 'Since you humiliated me through your elephant, you and the other devas may lose strength and energy,' he cursed.

This gave a chance to the asuras, the enemies of the devas, to attack Devlok under King Bali's leadership and win a great victory. Indra and his army went into hiding and prayed to Lord Vishnu, the preserver of the universe. 'Go and seek the nectar of immortality from the depths of the Ocean of Milk,' advised Lord Vishnu.

'How can we do that?' asked Indra.

'Churn the ocean with the help of the asuras. Be diplomatic and offer them half the nectar. Although,' said Lord Vishnu, 'I

will intervene at the last minute to ensure that the asuras don't get the nectar.'

As the devas and the asuras got ready to churn the ocean, they realised they needed a churning rod. Mount Meru, being the centre and axis of the world, was chosen to be that rod. Garuda brought the mountain to the ocean where the churning was to happen, and immediately flew away, so that the snake king, Vasuki, could act as the churning rope. Vasuki being a snake would never have gone near Mount Meru if Garuda was still hanging around, as Garuda preys on snakes.

As a result of its weight, Mount Mandhara started sinking into the ocean. To stop it from sinking, Lord Vishnu took the form of a giant tortoise, swam under the ocean and held up the mountain on his back.

While the devas held the tail of Vasuki, the asuras held the head of the snake. They continued to churn for many years. The massive churning caused Vasuki to release poisonous fumes from his head. They subsided after a while. Then a dangerous poison called *Halahal* emerged from the ocean that threatened to pollute the whole world. To save the world and stop the poison from spreading, Lord Shiva decided to drink it. This upset Shiva's wife, Parvati, who feared that the poison may affect her husband. So before the poison could reach Shiva's stomach, Parvati trapped it by gripping his neck with both her hands. The poison thus stayed in his throat, which is one of the reasons why Shiva's throat appears blue in some depictions. Another name for Lord Shiva is Neelkanth, the literal meaning of which is 'blue throat'.

After churning for millions of years, many things started to emerge from the ocean. Kamadhenu, the celestial cow, that gave whatever one asked for, was the one of the first beings to emerge. Vishnu gave Kamadhenu to the Sages for ghee and milk to be used for their rituals and sacrifices.

Then came Uchchaihshravas, a pristine white horse with seven heads. Uchchaihshravas could fly like Pegasus from Greek mythology. Then came Airavata, the elephant with four tusks, who became the vehicle of Lord Indra. Next came the Kausthubha gem, which Lord Vishnu wore around his neck. Then came the Kalpavriksha, which was a wish-fulfilling tree and was taken to heaven. Next came many apsaras, or heavenly dancers, like Rambha, Menaka and Punjikasthala, who were all taken to heaven.

Since everything that emerged so far had been taken to heaven, the asuras got annoyed. 'The next thing that comes out belongs to us,' they said. Varuni, the goddess of alcohol, emerged from the ocean. As agreed, Varuni was taken by the asuras who got drunk with the alcohol given by her.

Goddess Lakshmi emerged now, the custodian of wealth and fortune. Lord Vishnu accepted her as his wife because she garlanded him as soon as she rose from the ocean. Next came Chandrama, the moon god, whom Lord Shiva invited to adorn his head.

Panchajanya, a conch that emerged next, was taken by Lord Vishnu. The parijata tree which produced fragrant flowers that never wither was placed in Indra's home.

At last Lord Dhanvantari, who later became the physician of the devas, emerged. He carried a pot containing the immortal nectar. As soon as the devas and the asuras saw the pot, they started fighting.

To save the nectar from falling into the hands of the asuras, Lord Vishnu took the form of a beautiful woman, Mohini. Lord Vishnu as Mohini said, 'I am going to distribute the nectar to all of you. Please stand in a queue so that I don't miss out on anyone.'

The devas and the asuras formed two lines and Mohini started serving the devas first. Growing impatient, an asura called Rahu-Ketu joined the devas' line and managed to sip a drop of the immortal nectar.

When the sun and moon gods alerted Lord Vishnu of Rahu-Ketu changing his queue, Lord Vishnu used his Sudarshan Chakra to cut Rahu-Ketu in half. However, since Rahu-Ketu had consumed the immortal nectar, he did not die. His body was divided into two parts: the head was called Rahu and Ketu was the body. Rahu-Ketu thus nurtures an enmity with the sun and moon gods. It is said, Rahu swallows the sun and the moon at regular intervals, causing solar and lunar eclipses.

By the time the asuras realised Lord Vishnu's subtle game, the immortal nectar had been consumed in its entirety by the devas, who became immortal and strong. They went on to defeat the asuras.

This extraordinary story of the churning of the ocean is an invitation to reflect on ourselves, our potential that's as unlimited as the ocean, and the ability to regulate the good and the bad to achieve our goals.

How to maintain inner harmony?

There is a lot of symbolism in this story. During the churning of the ocean of milk, poison emerged first and then all the precious elements emerged. Finally the nectar of immortality came out. Similarly, during the stirring of our heart, the first things which come out may be our own negative baggages, but finally the nectar of immortality that feed the soul emerges. Even the churning of butter is a time-consuming task that requires patience. So to get something good in life, one has to be patient.
Lord Shiva did not hesitate in consuming poison to save the whole world from destruction. With such a selfless sacrifice, Nature also found a way to protect him.

Have Unshakeable Faith

The symbolism of the story

- This story represents the spiritual endeavour of human beings for gaining spiritual immortality through regulation of the mind, tempering of desires and the practice of meditation.
- The devas represent the pleasures of our lives, our senses and positivity.
- The asuras symbolise the pains, problems and negativity in our life.
- The ocean of milk signifies human consciousness.
- Mount Mandhara embodies human will used in meditation.
- The giant tortoise that held the mountain indicates divine grace which supports us.
- Vasuki, the serpent, represents desire. The devas and the asuras held the serpent and manipulated the pull, indicating regulation of desire to control the mind.
- Poison signifies challenges. When we begin any task, the first thing we encounter is a challenge.
- Lord Shiva embodies service and saccrifice, based on love. This is what eventually saved humanity.
- Treasures from the ocean indicate the short-lived temptations we succumb to in life. Do not get distracted by them, do not stop your efforts, till you attain your main goal or objective. Perseverance pays.
- Rahu-Ketu was rewarded with immortality, despite Lord Vishnu's many interventions. This shows that good and evil will continue to co-exist and true seekers should continue on their spiritual journey ignoring every other thing.
- Lord Vishnu as Mohini illustrates the imagination of the mind in the form of pride. Ego and pride are the last obstacles on a spiritual journey.

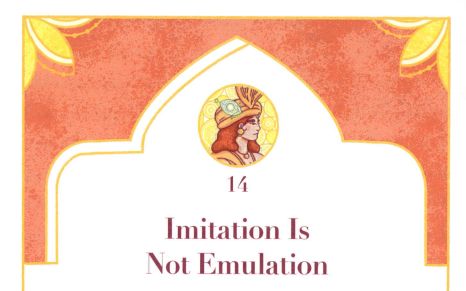

14

Imitation Is Not Emulation

King Paundraka Vasudeva believed himself to be Vasudeva or god and imitated Lord Krishna. His belief was strengthened by his self-serving courtiers who were mostly sycophants.

After Lord Krishna's victory over the mighty king of Magadha, Jarasandh, the world was talking about him. Paundraka, who admired Jarasandha, disliked the attention Krishna was getting. He lived in self-doubt and kept ignoring his royal duties. Observing his disinterest in governance, his ministers came up with a plan to get Paundraka out of inactivity. The courtiers started praising Paundraka and comparing him with Lord Krishna. 'You are a Vasudeva too. You are not merely a king but the lord of this universe,' they said.

King Paundraka started believing that he was a god, even greater than Lord Krishna. He started receiving guests, honours and gifts deserving of a god. His governors continued to praise the king and hinted that he was the rightful owner of all that belonged to Lord Krishna, even the Sudarshan Chakra (discus), the Kaumodaki (mace), the Saranga (bow) and the Nandaka (sword).

Imitation Is Not Emulation

But then one of the courtiers overdid his part. He said, 'Now it is just a matter of exposing the imposter, Krishna of Dwarka.'

'How do we do that?' asked Paundraka.

'Let's send an ambassador to Krishna's courts to tell him that the real god, Vasudeva, has revealed himself.'

Paundraka got carried away and said, 'Yes and he must return my weapons and my conch (Panchajanya).'

When Krishna heard Paundraka's directive, he laughed out aloud. The messenger continued, 'My lord Paundraka says that he would consider appointing you the governor of Dwarka if you let us annex it.'

Lord Krishna said, 'I shall forgive you as you are a mere messenger. I shall come and personally hand over my weapons.'

When the messenger relayed Krishna's words to Paundraka, the king was jubilant. He prepared for a big celebration. As soon as Krishna reached the kingdom of Pundra, Paundraka went to collect 'his' belongings.

To imitate Lord Krishna, Paundraka coloured his skin the same colour as Krishna's. He had the image of Garuda on his

chariot's flag, wore a yellow shawl just like Krishna, curled his hair like that of Krishna, wore the same type of garland around his neck, modelled the same crocodile-shaped earrings and even styled his chest like Krishna's Srivatsa (Vishnu's mark).

Seeing the imitation, Krishna laughed. This infuriated Paundraka who ordered his army to 'kill this imposter'. But the ever-vigilant Garuda swooped low and blew the weapons away.

'You asked for my weapons. I brought them. Do you want me to give them to you in my style?' Krishna asked calmly.

Krishna then hurled his mace towards Paundraka and blew his conch. The mace crashed into Paundraka's chariot, killing his charioteer and horses instantly.

'You wanted Nandaka, my sword, and Saranga, my bow. Here they are.' Saying this, Krishna hurled them both at Paundraka. The bow stopped mid-air, its string pulled taut. Krishna released his Sudarshan Chakra that aligned itself with the string of the bow, like a dart ready to be launched. Meanwhile, Nandaka, the sword, slayed Paundraka's army.

The Sudarshan Chakra released itself from the Saranga and slashed Paundraka's throat in a fraction of a second. As Paundraka closed his eyes, he saw the vision of the real god, Lord Krishna, in all his divine splendour. Thus ended the story of a king who made a parody of the lord.

How can we become like those who inspire us?

Meditation can change how we think, act and lead our lives, which may also create a more compassionate humanity. One can emulate the lifestyle of those who meditate and lead a wholesome life.

Emulate versus imitate

When Paundraka tried to imitate Lord Krishna, he copied only his external appearance and tried to confiscate his weapons. It was Paundraka's ego that blinded him towards the divine yogic powers of Krishna. The physical appearance is attractive and powerful, but transient. Copying this is not emulating and will not help us evolve.

The right way to emulate

The right way to emulate Lord Krishna is to improve one's yogic capacities. If Paundraka would have thought, Let me try to become divine like Krishna, he would have meditated and internalised the godly essence of Krishna. Then his consciousness would have become similar to Krishna's.

Emulate Those You Admire

Wisdom of emulating

When someone asked my spiritual guide, Babuji, 'How can I become like my guru?' He replied, 'Give your heart to god, and become restless for god.' He also said, 'Follow the teacher with wisdom.' He is emulating the inner qualities of the great person, systematically and steadily. Being aware of the difference between His level and ours creates humility and from there we improve.

15

The Fragrant Parijat Flowers

One day, the divine Sage Narada brought parijata flowers from the heavens and said, 'Oh Lord Krishna, I brought these fragrant flowers as a special offering to you.'

'How delightful! Let me give them to Rukmini,' said Krishna and he gave them to her.

Satyabhama, who is also Lord Krishna's wife, was offended. 'Lord, you know I adore parijata flowers. Yet you gave them to Rukmini.'

'Do not worry, my dear. Someday I shall get you the entire parijata tree,' replied Krishna.

Well, this incident was long forgotten and life went on as usual for Lord Krishna and his wives. However, it was not a good time for the gods in heaven. This was because of Narakasura, an asura who was torturing everyone and wreaking havoc everywhere. Lord Krishna and Satyabhama eventually killed Narakasura.

To celebrate Narakasura's death, Lord Indra invited Krishna and Satyabhama to his abode. After enjoying Lord Indra's hospitality for a few days, it was time for them to return home.

The Fragrant Parijat Flowers

As they were leaving, Satyabhama expressed her desire to have a tiny branch of the parijata tree so that she could plant it in Dwarka. A petty Indra refused as he could not bear to see another parijata tree bloom elsewhere.

Krishna wanted to teach Indra a lesson. So, he sent Garuda to get a branch of the tree. When Garuda returned with the branch, Satyabhama planted it, watered and look after the plant diligently and waited for it to flower. She planted it at the boundary of her and Rukmini's house. So, when the flowers bloomed, the branches leaned towards Rukmini's house and their perfume was carried towards the direction of Rukmini's house.

'Why doesn't my house smell of parijata flowers?' Satyabhama complained to Krishna.

Krishna laughed. 'It is no one's fault, my dear. The wind blows where it does. We cannot direct it.'

Satyabhama watered and loved the tree, but Rukmini was blessed by its perfume. Was it Satyabhama's fault that she did not get to enjoy the perfume of the parijata flowers? Was it the wind's fault? Nature has its choices and preferences. We have to accept them with a smile. Then life will be simpler and happier.

What are we really attracted to when we are drawn to certain people?

Bees can locate a flower hidden between crevices or lost inside thick foliage, which our human eye cannot detect. Have you wondered how that is possible?

The quintessence of life

Just like the bees' ability to detect nectar from flowers hidden from us, there are many phenomena in Nature that instil awe and wonder. Although there is no proof that swans can separate milk from water, scientists have recently discovered a sieve-like structure in their mouths that allows them to separate mud from water. There are so many natural phenomena where things are sought with focus, precision and intent. The quintessence of our lives is the subconscious choices that we make.

Seek the Essence

The relationship between a guru and disciple

Even in the interactions between the spiritual master and his disciples, we often notice that there are some who spend a lot of personal time with him, physically enjoying his company. This is analogous to seeking a branch of the parijata tree. There are also others who receive the spiritual essence of the guru. These disciples could be far away, across oceans. They empty their mind, open their heart, and wait patiently, receiving the grace of the lord, the spiritual perfume of the guru.

The imagery of the parijata tree

Only when you experience the essence of a spiritual transformation, can you appreciate the work of a spiritual master. The first time I came across this story, I was instantly attracted to the imagery of the parijata tree and its analogy with my own spiritual teacher, Babuji. I have met him a few times. Babuji met his spiritual teacher, Lalaji, hardly a few times, yet Babuji became Lalaji's spiritual successor. The guru's presence is very attractive, but it is his yogic transmission, or pranahuti, that can transform our character.

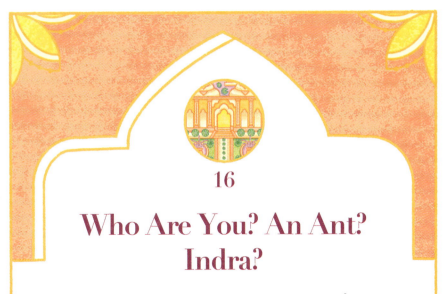

16

Who Are You? An Ant? Indra?

Vritrasura was a mighty asura who wreaked havoc on the devas. He destroyed Devlok, the kingdom of Indra. That was when Indra asked Sage Dadhichi to sacrifice his life so that he could construct his thunderbolt weapon from his bones. After killing Vritrasura with that weapon, he undertook the task of rebuilding Devlok.

To help with this task, Indra summoned Vishwakarma, the divine architect. 'Please reconstruct our palaces and make Devlok as beautiful as it once was.'

Vishwakarma was a smart architect and he rebuilt Devlok with astonishing palaces, sparkling lakes and tall towers. But Indra was not satisfied and wanted more improvements.

So Vishwakarma continued rebuilding. With every year of work, Indra's demands only increased. Finally, a frustrated Vishwakarma approached Brahma for help: 'Only you can save me from this. I cannot seem to please Indra.'

'Don't worry, dear Vishwakarma,' assured the Creator. 'Tomorrow your task shall be completed.' But Brahma was not sure how to help Vishwakarma. So he went to Lord Vishnu, the supreme being of the universe.

When Vishnu smiled, Brahma understood that Vishnu would take care of it. So Brahma returned to Brahma-lok.

The next morning, a young boy carrying a staff and a tiny umbrella appeared at the gates of Indra's palace. 'I would like to meet Lord Indra,' he said to one of the gatekeepers.

The boy exuded wisdom and inspired reverence. When the gatekeepers informed Indra of the young boy, Indra was curious and asked them to bring him in. When Indra saw the boy, he felt compelled to bow. Indra then asked, 'What do you seek from me, young one?'

'Your Devlok is beautiful,' replied the young boy. 'I heard that Vishwakarma is rebuilding it. I wanted to see it myself.'

Indra was vain and full of pride. 'Behold the most beautiful construction in the whole universe.'

'I have a few questions for you,' the young boy said.

'Ask, my dear boy.'

'How many years will you continue to build Devlok?' What further engineering and scientific feats is Vishwakarma going to accomplish?'

Indra laughed. 'Do you think it is a small thing? Have you seen anything like this city before? How many Indras and Vishvakarmas have you seen? How many do you even know of?'

'I know your father, Prajapati Kashyapa, and your grandfather Marichi, who was born from Brahma's mind. I also know Brahma's father Vishnu, from whose navel Brahma was born. And I saw the dissolution of the universe, the great mahapralaya, when the universe sank into a great void. I have seen the recreation of the universe. I have also seen the dissolution of an infinite number of universes and their recreation. They all have their own Brahmas, Vishnus and Shivas. Who can count them? Who can count the number of Indras who succeed every other Indra?'

The young boy continued. 'An Indra lives merely for a few yugas. And when twenty-eight Indras have taken birth and died, a mere day and night in the life of a Brahma elapses. In Brahma-

years, a Brahma's life is only 108. One Brahma succeeds the other. How can I count the Indras, now?

'Eggs of Brahma float on the pure water that forms the body of Vishnu. And from every pore of Lord Vishnu, a new universe emerges. Do I even dare to count the universes? How can I count the Indras then?'

Indra was astounded into silence. The boy glanced down at his feet to see an army of ants marching in a matrix and laughed.

'Why do you laugh?' asked Indra, 'Who are you? You seem to be a wise Sage in the guise of a young boy.'

'I am no Sage,' the boy said. 'And I laughed looking at these ants and the reason for my laughter is a secret.'

'Pray, tell me the secret,' Indra requested.

'Each of the ants was an Indra in a previous birth,' replied the young boy. 'Each one was virtuous and lived in the human form. They lived, died and committed benevolent deeds for humanity and through the cycle of births and deaths, they are now in the form of ants.

'Good and bad deeds allow us to either elevate ourselves to the glorious realms of the heavens as Indras or other gods,' the boy continued, 'or sink us into pain and suffering respectively. These deeds allow us to be born as human beings, animals, birds and reptiles through vast cycles of births and deaths. All these are just one's karma.'

He concluded: 'A wise person is attached neither to grandeur, like your magnificent palaces and mansions, nor to the life of an ant. When a wise person gets that wisdom, he is absolved of karma.'

Indra was humbled listening to the young boy. The next day, he let Vishwakarma conclude the architectural task and go home.

What is karma?

Whatever a man sows, he will reap, suggests the Bible. In India, karma is a widely accepted idea. The Bhagwad Gita also advocates this.

Karma is action

Karma does not simply mean your fate is fixed. The word karma stands for action not fate. Action and intention are the laws of life. Without action, it is not possible to exist and without intention, it is not possible to exert the willpower that is needed to act. Karma is an energy created by wilful thought and action. It simply indicates that we have the freedom to decide what happens to us eventually and that our lives are an outcome of our willpower and intention.

Karma Is an Energy Created from Our Actions and Thoughts

Designing your own destiny

It is a misunderstanding that we are not in control of our destiny. We can change our intentions and rewire our pathways. We give up and do not change when we fail to exert our willpower. Observe yourself and see how you react to situations. Think about how your thoughts and actions affect your karmic energy.

Water the garden of your mind

Our energy takes control of our lives. If we feel angry, sad or discontent, these energies dominate our actions. In this story, the young boy helped Lord Indra replace the seeds of insecurity, vanity and ego with the seeds of humility and contentment. The ants helped Indra change his perspective. Life always gives us experiences that are helpful for the evolution of our consciousness and if we are attentive, we can live a purposeful life.

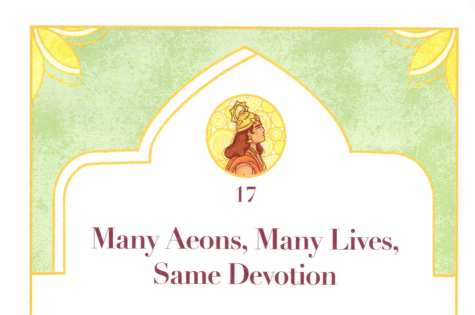

17
Many Aeons, Many Lives, Same Devotion

In the Ramayana, Lord Rama came back to Ayodhya after defeating Ravana in Lanka. As king of Ayodhya, his rule was termed Rama-rajya, meaning, the kingdom where peace, joy and contentment reigned and the subjects flourished.

However, after years, the gods felt that Lord Rama should return as Lord Vishnu to his abode in Vaikuntha. So the gods approached Yama, the lord of death, to take away Rama's life.

Rama knew that Yama couldn't take away his life because Rama's favourite disciple, Hanuman, was guarding Rama's life.

'I must trick Hanuman,' Rama thought. 'Otherwise, Yama will never be able to take my life.'

One day, Lord Rama dropped his ring into a crack on the floor. He asked Hanuman to retrieve his ring. Hanuman had the powers to transmute his body to the smallest or the largest size possible. So he shrunk himself to the size of an ant and jumped into the crack but could not find the ring. He went deeper into the depths of the earth till he reached Patal-lok, or the netherworld.

In Patal-lok, Hanuman met the king of snakes, Vasuki. He asked Vasuki if he had seen Lord Rama's ring.

'Yes, it is here. Come with me,' Vasuki said, beckoning Hanuman into a room that was full of rings like that of Rama's. 'How will I find Lord Rama's ring from among all these rings?'

'You can take any ring from here,' Vasuki said. 'They all belong to Rama.'

'How?' asked a confused Hanuman.

'Each ring represents a chatur-yuga (four yugas), which is a unit of time in the kal-chakra (wheel of time),' Vasuki said. 'The four yugas are Satya Yuga, Treta Yuga, Dwapara Yuga and Kali Yuga. During every Treta

Yuga, a Rama and a Hanuman are born. And every time Lord Rama drops his ring, Hanuman comes down to the Patal-lok to look for it. By the time Hanuman returns with the ring, Lord Rama returns as Lord Vishnu to Vaikuntha. So all these rings do belong to Lord Rama, each one from the different ages the universe was created and destroyed. You can take any of the rings back to Lord Rama.'

Hanuman understood what he was implying and prayerfully let go of his dear lord. He thanked Vasuki and returned.

Meanwhile, in Hanuman's absence, Lord Rama arranged for the coronation of his sons, Prince Lav and Prince Kush. It was time for him to go. He entered the Sarayu river and gave up his life.

No one can stop death, not even avatars. One who is born, lives and dies. Even Hanuman, known as one of the chiranjeevis, meaning one who is eternal, had to die eventually after the kalpa, or eon, ended.

What is the point of life, death and beyond?

Before we came here, there may have been many like us. There may be many after us too. The concept of life and death is unique and timeless, illustrating the cyclical nature of time. When it is time to die, even gods are not spared.

Life, death and beyond

Life, death and beyond are interconnected concepts central to human existence. They inspire curiosity, wonder and reflection and they continue to shape the way we live our lives and view the world around us. It is natural to feel afraid or anxious about death because it is an inevitable part of life that can be difficult to comprehend.

Only the Present Matters, Be in Joy

Live a purposeful existence

Engaging in activities that are meaningful can help give our lives a sense of purpose and fulfilment. Whether it's learning a new skill, a new language, volunteering, pursuing a creative passion or spending time with loved ones, when we focus on what matters most to us, we are not affected by death or beyond. We can choose to live purposefully in the present. By focusing on living life to the fullest, we move away from the uncertainty of the beyond. Drafting a list of favourite activities and creative passions can lead to living a purposeful life.

Devotion and a joyful life

Hanuman was so devoted to Lord Rama that his presence gave Lord Rama protection from the Lord of Death. Lord Rama had to play a trick on Hanuman for him to leave. There is nothing wrong with Hanuman's devotion, in fact it is commendable.

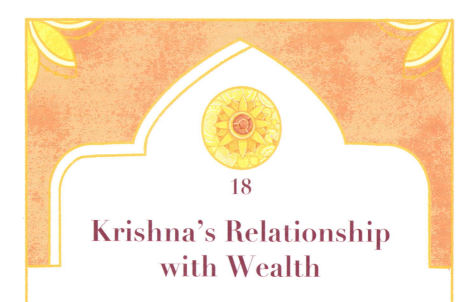

18

Krishna's Relationship with Wealth

Satrajit, an aristocrat from Dwarka, once prayed to Lord Surya, the sun god. Pleased with Satrajit's devotion, Surya gave him the magical gem, Syamanthaka, as a gift. The Syamanthaka was famed to give eight measures of gold every day to its keeper.

So the already rich Satrajit became wealthier. Seeing Satrajit's wealth grow, Lord Krishna said to him, 'It would be good to share your wealth with Dwarka. Please give the gem to King Ugrasena as he can use it for the development of our country.'

But Satrajit declined.

One day, Satrajit's brother Prasena went hunting wearing the Syamanthaka gem around his neck on a chain. There he climbed a tree to wait for some wild animals to pass through the forest. A lion approached the tree and just when Prasena was about to shoot an arrow a snake dropped from above, making Prasena lose his balance. Consequently, his chain became entangled in a tree branch, strangling him to death.

The bright and attractive gem caught the lion's attention. He walked away with the Syamanthaka gem to his cave. Jambavan, the king of the bears, saw the lion carrying the gem. Attracted to the gem, Jambavan attacked the lion, killing him instantly. Jambavan then gave the gem to his infant son.

Meanwhile, when Prasena did not return to Dwarka, Satrajit suspected Lord Krishna of foul play. To prove his innocence, Krishna embarked into the forest to find Prasena and the gem. Krishna found Prasena's dead body in the jungle and noticed the lion's tracks circling away from it. Then he followed the lion's tracks to its cave. There he saw the dead lion, its body ripped apart with claws. Bear tracks surrounded the body and were leading away. He followed the tracks, until he reached Jambavan's cave.

Krishna saw Jambavan's son playing with the Syamanthaka. Startled by the stranger, the child started crying, alerting Jambavan, who attacked Krishna. They fought for twenty-eight days, after which Jambavan realised the divinity of Krishna. He understood that Krishna was the next avatar just like Lord Rama was the previous avatar of Lord Vishnu. Jambavan was a devotee of Lord Ram. 'Please forgive me and accept my daughter Jambavati as your wife,' said Jambavan. Lord Krishna accepted Jambavati as his wife.

Lord Krishna returned to Dwarka with the Syamanthaka gem and his new bride. He returned the gem to its rightful owner. Seeing Krishna's benevolence, Satrajit offered his daughter Satyabama as a wife to Lord Krishna and he accepted. Satrajit also offered the Syamanthaka, but Lord Krishna refused.

Before her wedding to Krishna, Satyabama was pursued by other suitors. Those suitors did not like Satrajit offering Satyabama to Lord Krishna. So one of them, Shatadhanwa, killed Satrajit, stole the Syamanthaka, gave it to another suitor, Akrura, for safekeeping and ran away.

Shatadhanwa was caught and punished by Krishna and his brother, Balarama. They soon realised that Shatadhanwa had passed on the gem to Akrura. Upon prodding, Akrura confessed that Shatadhanwa had given him the gem for safekeeping. Krishna then advised Akrura: 'Tell the inhabitants of Dwarka the truth about the gem. Otherwise, they will suspect you of murdering Satrajit. Since he was a gentleman of Dwarka, the crime will have grave punishment.' Akrura had the wisdom to listen to Lord Krishna. So when Akrura confessed his crime, Krishna let him keep the Syamanthaka gem on the condition that it did not leave Dwarka.

So the gem of Dwarka stayed in Dwarka.

What can wealth teach us?

Wealth and riches can corrupt relatives and friends, making them enemies. If Satrajit would have used the jewel for the well-being of Dwarka then lives would have been saved.

Handling wealth

'With great power comes great responsibility,' says Spiderman in the Marvel movies. Similarly, with wealth comes the duty to use it wisely and not to get caught up in its glamour. Handling wealth is about responsibility and using it wisely to benefit not only ourselves but also others.

Generosity and responsibility

Sharing wealth with others can be charitable giving, volunteering or other forms of philanthropy. When you share your lunch with a hungry friend or teach a friend struggling with studies, it can do him good. It is altruistic. Use wealth and resources responsibly.

Responsibility and Restraint

Wealth can affect personality

One must stay balanced and realise that wealth, money and material possessions merely facilitate a comfortable life. So it would be prudent to avoid arrogance or conceit about possessing wealth, which is merely a resource. Avoid acts that compromise integrity and affect our character.

Spirituality and wealth

Be grateful for what is given to you. Recognize that your wealth is not solely the result of your efforts but also the contributions of others. Wealth is not the goal of life but a means to happiness and comfort. Think of the consequences of unethical or immoral acts.

19

Power of Pause and Poise

Once upon a time, there was a great ruler called Ambarish. He and his wife were down to earth, humble and god-loving people. He was popular with all—Sages, spiritual leaders, his subjects and even the devas. Under the guidance of spiritual Sages like Vasishta and Gautama, Ambarish performed a special sacrificial ritual where he donated riches. Lord Vishnu was pleased with him and said, 'I offer you my powerful Sudarshan Chakra as protection. No asuras or enemy can attack you now.'

Once during the course of their reign, while Ambarish and his wife were on a special fast, the legendary Sage Durvasa, known for his short temper, arrived at Ambarish's kingdom. The king and his wife were about to break their fast and so invited the Sage to dine with them. Durvasa said, 'Let me bathe in the River Yamuna and then I shall have food with you.' While bathing, Sage Durvasa entered a deep meditative state and lost track of time. The king knew it was disrespectful to eat without the Sage but the auspicious time for breaking the fast was nearing.

'Oh wise sages, what shall we do now?' he asked those who were present.

'You may drink water. According to the Vedas, drinking water is equivalent to breaking the fast. It is also equivalent to waiting for Durvasa to eat food. That way, we will appease the gods and still show respect to Sage Durvasa.'

The king drank a cup of water and broke his fast. When Sage Durvasa returned from his bath, he came to know about it and his temper flared immediately. 'How dare you defy dharma! You are vain and proud because of your wealth. You invited me as a guest, but you broke your fast before feeding me. Is it right to eat before the guest? The Vedas say, "Atithi devo bhava" meaning, the guest is like god. I am going to punish you for this act of disrespect.'

Durvasa pulled out a strand of his hair and created a female demon. She spewed fire like a dragon, pulled out her sword and charged at Ambarish who displayed no fear. He knew no harm would come to him.

The Sudarshan Chakra that had been delegated to protect Ambarish by Lord Vishnu appeared instantaneously and destroyed the female demon. The Sudarshan Chakra then turned toward Durvasa since he was the source of the demon. The Sudarshan Chakra chased Durvasa. The Sage ran across mountains, dived deep into the sea, leapt high into the sky but it chased him everywhere. Durvasa appealed to Lord Brahma, the creator, for help.

'Lord Vishnu is like a father to me,' said Brahma. 'I was born from his navel. I bow to his command. How can I stop his weapon?'

Durvasa then sought refuge from Lord Shiva, who said, 'How can I even think of defying Lord Vishnu or his weapon? He has given birth to thousands of Brahmas and millions of universes. Go and seek asylum from Lord Vishnu himself.'

When Durvasa arrived at Vaikuntha, Vishnu's abode, he fell on his feet, 'Please forgive me, my Lord. I was ignorant and arrogant. I offended your disciple. Please recall your weapon and save me.'

Lord Vishnu then said, 'What can I do? My disciples command me. Their love makes me their humble servant. How can I

abandon them? You are here because you offended Ambarish. Go and seek his forgiveness. Perhaps the Sudarshan Chakra will then forgive you. Knowledge and piety are held in high esteem. But never forget that love of a disciple for the disciple is dear to the Lord.'

Durvasa then left.

Finally, Durvasa returned to the kingdom with the Sudarshan Chakra following close behind. He fell at Ambarish's feet, 'Forgive me,' he said, 'Please recall the Sudarshan Chakra.'

'Oh Sudarshan Chakra, please spare Sage Durvasa,' Ambarish beseeched, showing deep compassion and respect. 'You love the Lord's disciples as much as he does. Please accept my request and forgive Durvasa.'

Immediately, the Sudarshan Chakra stopped chasing the sage. A long time had elapsed since Durvasa had first visited Ambarish. He was still waiting patiently for Duruva to break his fast.

So now, they sat down to dine together, and afterwards, Sage Durvasa blessed Ambarish and took leave of him.

In this story, we see King Ambarish's strength of devotion to the lord. We see his forbearance, patience and humility. We also notice how anger is not a good thing. King Ambarish's life has a very valuable lesson about spiritual poise.

How to avoid overreacting

To pause when you feel angry takes practice and effort. Pausing and waiting may solve many problems though, at times, immediate corrective action is also required.

The power of pause

Durvasa paid for his short temper. If Durvasa had waited for Ambarish to tell him why he broke his fast, how do you think the story would have evolved? It is good to practise the 'power of pause' when overcome with sudden emotion. Decision-making is effective when we are in a non-reactive mode. When our disposition is cool and calm, we will always act for the good of all.

What is spiritual poise?

Spiritual poise involves having a deep sense of inner peace, confidence and a connection with a divine force. It is the ability to stay grounded in the face of challenges and to draw upon one's own spiritual strength and wisdom. Spiritual poise is valuable and can help develop resilience, inner strength and a sense of fulfilment. In this story, King Ambarish shows spiritual poise.

Maintain Spiritual Poise

How to develop spiritual poise?

If not for Durvasa's anger, we may not have known about King Ambarish's spiritual poise. There is a purpose in everything—both good and bad. When we have faith in the process of life, life becomes beautiful. That is the beginning of spiritual poise. It can be cultivated through meditation. As soon as you wake up, sit down for a few minutes and focus on the goodness and love in your heart. You will develop a sense of equanimity and a deeper understanding of yourself and your place in the world.

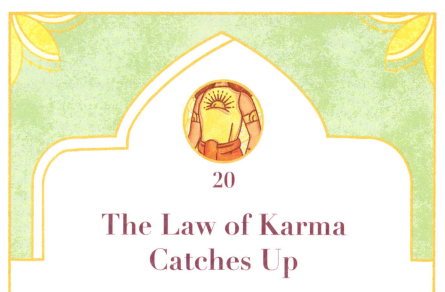

20

The Law of Karma Catches Up

Nara and Narayana were twins born to Dharma and Murti and were the incarnations of Lord Vishnu. Lord Krishna and Arjuna from the Mahabharata were believed to be incarnations of these two Sages.

Nara and Narayana grew up in their parents' ashram and learned the scriptures and the art of warfare and practised meditation from an early age. Lord Shiva, the destroyer of the universe, decided to test Nara and Narayana. When Shiva launched his weapon Pashupatastra at them, it lost its potency because their meditation was so deep and powerful.

Lord Vishnu had incarnated as Nara and Narayana to save the earth from a formidable asura called Dambhodbhava. Dambhodbhava prayed for many years to the sun god, Lord Surya, for the boon of immortality.

Surya said it was impossible to give this boon as even the gods had to perish at the dissolution of the universe. To circumvent mortality, a smart Dambhodbhava requested, 'Give me the protection of Sahasra-kavacha, or a thousand armours, with the condition that in any battle each armour could be destroyed by only that warrior who has meditated for a thousand years. Also, if the same warrior had to remove the second armour, he would have to go back and meditate for another thousand years, and so on.' Added to this protection was the last clause—if a warrior removes one of the armours, that warrior should fall dead immediately.

Since this boon did not involve immortality, Lord Surya could not refuse and called Dambhodbhava 'Sahasra-kavacha', meaning 'one who has a thousand armours'.

The last clause in the boon was the catch. Nobody wanted to challenge Sahasra-kavacha as they knew they would die. So Sahasra-kavacha captured the entire world, annexed kingdoms and challenged all. Earth was having a tough time. Everyone prayed to the Creator. Lord Brahma knew that none could destroy Sahasra-kavacha. So to trick him he said, 'Why don't you challenge the twin Sages, Nara and Narayana?'

So Sahasra-kavacha reached the ashram of these two Sages. Narayana had just completed a thousand years of penance and Nara had just sat down for his thousand years of penance. Since Narayana had fulfilled the conditions granted to fight Sahasra-kavacha, he easily removed one of *Sahasra-kavacha's* thousand armours. But then Narayana died, as was stated in the last clause of the boon. However, Nara immediately revived his brother using the Mrityunjay mantra, which can bring someone back to life. Narayana then went to meditate for another thousand years.

Now Nara fought Sahasra-kavacha and removed one more of his armours but had to die, like his brother. By this time, Narayana had completed another thousand years of meditation and immediately brought Nara back to life using the same mantra. This process continued until the brothers had removed 999 of Sahasra-kavacha's armours.

Now only one armour remained. It was Nara's turn. Sahasra-kavacha knew if Nara removed this last armour, he would die. So Sahasra-kavacha sought asylum with Lord Surya, who did not hand him over to Nara as it was against his dharma.

The kalpa, or the time cycle of creation, was ending. Maha pralaya, or the complete dissolution of the universe, was about to commence. Even though Sahasra-kavacha had escaped, he had to be reborn because of his karma. So in the next yuga, Sahasra-kavacha was reborn with his single armour as Karna. In this incarnation, Lord Surya was Karna's father.

In their next incarnation, Nara and Narayan were born as Arjuna and Lord Krishna. It was Nara's turn to kill Dambhodbhava. So Arjuna killed Karna at Kurukshetra during the Mahabharata war, with Lord Krishna serving as his charioteer.

In this incarnation, Arjuna's father, Lord Indra, watched over his son. He knew that if Arjuna removed Karna's armour, Arjuna would die as per the boon. So Indra disguised himself as a beggar and asked for Karna's armour, as alms. Karna, being exceedingly generous, gave away his armour, knowing it would mean death at the hands of Arjuna. The Mahabharata war was won by Arjuna and his brothers with the help of Lord Krishna.

Today, the world knows Karna for his generosity, bravery and honesty. Karna was one of the most powerful warriors at Kurukshetra. The difficulties he faced in his life, the insults he experienced, were all because of his past life as Dambhodbhava when he made humanity suffer.

The greatness of Karna and the valour of Nara and Narayana are inspiring. Our past actions always catch up and we are accountable for whatever we do. Whether it's immediate or in another life, the law of karma always catches up.

How to create positive outcomes in spite of the theory of karma

Karma is energy created because of our actions and thoughts. What we sow, we reap. So does everyone who commit a right or wrong. They have to undergo the repercussions of their actions. But is there a way out?

The spiritual idea

If Sahasra-kavacha had been a good human being, he could have avoided the suffering as Karna, and in that next kalpa, his soul would have evolved into a higher being. His life would have been more useful then. It is better to be free of karma as early as possible and to be liberated from the cycle of life and death.

Change of heart

The phrase 'change of heart' means a significant shift in attitudes and beliefs. When emotional baggage is removed, there is a quick change of heart. When this happens, the heart becomes more compassionate, loving and tender. Then the karma creates a different destiny.

Keep Your Heart Light and Clean

The practical manifestation of karma, destiny and potency

Destiny, karma and potency are all interesting spiritual ideas. As youngsters, how can we make sense of this in our life? You must understand that every action has a reaction. So always try to do good, think good thoughts and manifest only goodness. But at times, we do make mistakes. It is wise to learn from mistakes, ask for forgiveness and not repeat them again.

21

May Noble Thoughts Come from Everywhere

Among the seven sacred sages called saptarishis, there was an extraordinary Sage called Atri. His wife Anasuya was devoted to him. One day, the wives of Lord Brahma, Lord Vishnu and Lord Shiva decided to test Anasuya. They told their husbands, 'Why don't you test the wisdom, devotion and modesty of Anasuya?'

So the gods disguised themselves as monks and went down to Earth and asked for alms from Anasuya. 'We have a condition. You have to be unclothed while you give us food,' they told Anasuya.

Anasuya was not only spiritual and wise but also had a lot of common sense. She just smiled and said, 'So be it.' With her spiritual powers, she made the three adult monks into babies and unclothed herself and fed them food.

When her husband came home and saw three babies playing at home, he was delighted the gods had decided to visit him. In his joy, he hugged the three babies. But when he hugged them, the three babies became one baby.

In the celestial world, the wives of the gods, goddess Lakshmi, goddess Parvati and goddess Saraswati, were waiting for their husbands to return. When they didn't come back for a long time, they came down to Earth to check. They were surprised to witness a mere mortal, Anasuya, reduce the gods to babies. They requested Anasuya to return their husbands as they had celestial roles to play, but she refused.

'I want to keep the baby. I feel like their mother,' she said. So the gods then decided to leave a part of themselves as a single baby—Anasuya's son—and returned to their heavenly abode. This baby grew up to become Sage Dattatreya. He was a celestial miracle as he was a part of the Trinity.

Dattatreya grew up to be wise and learned. He was peaceful, contented and friendly. Because of these qualities, people followed him everywhere. In need of some privacy and solitude, one day he entered a huge lake and went into a deep meditative state, samadhi. When he came out after three days, people were still waiting for him at the lake.

To get rid of this distracting crowd, and in pursuit of solitude, Dattatreya created a beautiful girl and gave her a pitcher of wine. When people saw

Dattatreya with the girl, they thought he had been corrupted. They immediately left him. His purpose was served.

With time, Dattatreya gave away all his belongings and started living like a mendicant, while at the same time he continued his spiritual work. It is said that during this period, even the great warrior god Karthikeya learnt the Avadhuta Gita (The Gita of self-realisation) from Dattatreya.

When Dattatreya was thus wandering around peacefully he met King Yadu.

'What is the secret of your happiness?' asked King Yadu.

'There is no secret,' replied Dattatreya.

'I have everything, yet I am unhappy. You have nothing, yet you are joyous. Who is your guru?' asked King Yadu.

'The god within is my guru, and he teaches through many outer gurus,' replied Dattatreya.

'Please teach me too how to arrive at such realisations,' asked King Yadu.

So Dattatreya taught King Yadu some of the teachings which came to be known as Avadhuta Gita. Yadu was inspired by the Avadhuta Gita and inculcated its teachings in his everyday life to become a successful ruler.

Sage Dattatreya's Teachings for King Yadu

From the Earth, I learnt how to be patient, tolerant and unprejudiced. The Earth always does good, even to those who do bad.

From the water, I learnt the quality of nourishment and cleanliness. I cleanse away greed, lust, selfishness and egoism.

A male elephant runs after the smell of a female elephant and falls in the pit and gets trapped. When I saw this happen, I learnt not to fall into the traps of sensory gratification.

From the air, I learnt how to move on from situations and people, without getting emotionally attached.

Bees collect honey and hoard it in their hive only for the hunter to set fire to it. We also hoard wealth only to leave it behind when we die. From this, I learnt not to hoard.

From the fire, I learnt to burn bright with the light of knowledge and goodness. I also learnt how to reform and purify all.

The bees suck honey from different flowers. Similar to them I learnt to seek a small amount of food from many houses instead of being a burden on any single family.

From the sky, I learnt that my real higher self is infinite. The sky is unaffected by thunderstorms and lightning. I learnt to be unaffected by anything that comes my way.

The moon appears to wax and wane, giving us the perception of growing and shrinking when in reality it is full and whole. I learnt that I am also full and whole in spite of many births and deaths.

From the python, I learnt contentment. It does not go in search of food but is content to eat whatever comes its way.

The sun is reflected in puddles as numerous suns but is intrinsically one. From this, I learnt that the highest self is only one even though it appears to be many.

A few baby pigeons got trapped in a hunter's net. The parent pigeons voluntarily followed their children into the net. I learnt that attachment is the cause of bondage and suffering.

He learnt many things from nature directly

The deer is frightened by hearing the drums of hunters and falls in a trap. From this, I learnt not to succumb to the stress and pressures created by others.

When a moth is attracted by the flame, it burns itself up and dies. From this I learnt to practise caution and not get attracted by glamour.

The fish is lured by the bait, gets caught and dies. From this, I learnt not to be caught in the allure of crumbs. Greed for tasty food must be avoided.

A snake sheds its old skin when it is time. From this I learnt that a saint can give up old ideas when the time comes.

When an archer is so focused on the bullseye, he did not notice even a king's huge procession. I learnt that if I can meditate with such focus, it will lead me to self-realisation.

All the rivers empty into the ocean and cause ripples. But the deepest part of the ocean is very still. From this, I learnt not to be disturbed by sensory inputs but keep my mind still.

Insects get trapped in a spider's web but the spider does not. It also abandons the web when the time comes. From this, I learnt not to get entangled in the world of events and to give them up in time.

When a hawk picks up a piece of meat, it is attacked by other birds. I learnt that similarly, a person is not peaceful when he seeks sensory pleasures in life.

The caterpillar is enclosed in its cocoon and waits till it becomes a butterfly. Seeing this, I also learnt to wait patiently till I can fly out with my success.

An infant drinks milk and is free of all worries. I also learnt to live in the present.

When artists don't get appreciation they get disappointed. But when they have no expectation they immerse themselves in their art. From this I learnt to contribute with no expectations.

The bangles of a young girl jingled and gathered unwanted attention. She broke all but one bangle to stop receiving attention. Similarly, a yogi should avoid unnecessary attention and meditate by himself.

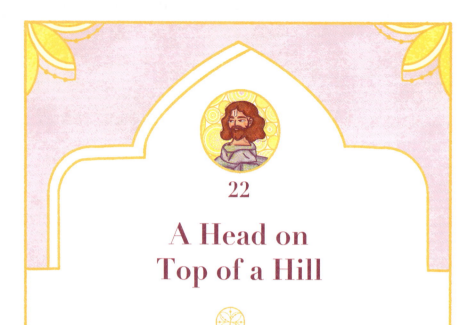

22

A Head on Top of a Hill

Once upon a time, the devas went to Vaikuntha, the abode of Lord Vishnu, and complained to him about the increase in the number of cruel people. It was then that Lord Vishnu decided to incarnate as Krishna and vanquish the wicked and bring peace to Earth.

Though most devas were happy with this solution, one yaksha said, 'Why disturb Lord Vishnu? I can single-handedly destroy all evil in the world at one go.'

Hearing this conversation between the yaksha and the devas, Brahma, the Creator, got offended because it implied that he and the devas were not valiant enough and that the devas had disturbed Lord Vishnu for nothing. He also thought the yaksha was egoistic and arrogant. So Brahma cursed the yaksha, 'Lord Vishnu will incarnate on Earth and kill you first. Only after that will he kill the wicked.'

So this yaksha was born as Barbarik, the grandson of Bhima, who was the second of the five Pandava brothers. Barbarik was the son of Ghatotkacha and Ahiliwati who was a great warrior.

She taught him the art of warfare. To please Lord Shiva, Barbarik meditated for many years and finally Shiva bestowed him with three special arrows.

In the war of Kurukshetra, the Pandavas and the Kauravas fought for the throne of Hastinapur. Before the battle began, Ahiliwati asked her son to join the side that was weaker at any point during the war.

Since Lord Krishna knew Barbarik was the strongest warrior among all those at Kurukshetra, he wanted him out of the war. So he tricked Barbarik. He first asked Bhishma, the paternal elder of the Kuru dynasty, 'How many days do you think it would take you to finish this war all by yourself?'

'I would take twenty days,' replied Bhishma.

'How many days do you think you would take to defeat everyone?' Krishna asked Dronacharya, the teacher of the Kauravas and the Pandavas.

'I would take twenty-five days,' replied Drona.

'Now how many days would you take, Arjuna?' asked Krishna.

'I would take twenty-eight days,' replied Arjuna.

When Krishna asked Barbarik, he said, 'Less than an hour.'

'How do you intend to do that?' asked Krishna.

'I have three special arrows and I can end the war with their unique powers,' replied Barbarik. 'With the first arrow, I will mark those I need to destroy. With the second, I will mark those I want to save and with the third, I will destroy those that I marked first,' he continued.

'I do not believe you. I wonder if your arrows can even remove all the leaves from this tree,' Krishna challenged him, pointing to the tree under which they were standing.

'I can do that,' said Barbarik, and sat down under the tree to meditate.

While Barbarik was deep in meditation, Krishna plucked a

small green leaf and hid it under his foot. After praying to Lord Shiva, Barbarik requested the arrows to do their job. The first arrow released itself and marked all the leaves on the tree and then swooped low, near Krishna's feet.

'Why is this arrow floating in the air, just above my foot?' asked Krishna, feigning innocence.

'Perhaps there is a leaf under your foot,' replied Barbarik. 'Please lift your feet and let the arrow check underneath'.

As Krishna lifted his foot, the first arrow marked the leaf that Krishna had hidden under his feet. The third arrow now pierced all the leaves on the tree, marked by the first arrow. Krishna was spellbound by Barbarik's powers.

'Your arrows are indeed infallible,' Krishna said. 'Tell me, whom are you going to support in the Kurukshetra war?'

'I have promised my mother I would support the weaker side,' replied Barbarik. 'Since my grandfather's side, the Pandavas, have fewer warriors I am going to fight on their side'.

'Your promise to your mother seems like a paradox to me,' said Krishna. 'If you support the Pandavas thinking that they are the weaker side, they will become the stronger side because of your special powers.'

'Yes, that's the idea,' said Barbarik.

'But then this will make the Kauravas the weaker side,' Krishna pointed out,' and you will have to switch sides again because of the same logic. This way you will keep oscillating between the two sides through the war. That would then be a transgression of the code of ethics of war. Also, you would end up killing both sides as and when you switch sides and you will be the only one alive.'

Then Krishna informed Barbarik of the tradition followed just before the start of a war, where the bravest warrior's head is offered as a sacrifice to obtain victory. 'May I seek yours as you are the mightiest of them all?' requested Krishna.

Barbarik agreed but had one condition: He wanted to watch the Kurukshetra war fully.

Krishna agreed. 'I shall dip your head in nectar, or the eternal life-giving amrit, and place it on top of the hill situated at the edge of the battlefield.'

So after sacrificing his head, Barbarik watched the whole Kurukshetra war from the head kept on the hilltop. With this, Brahma's curse on the yaksha was fulfilled. As prophesied in the curse, the yaksha reborn as Barbarik was killed before the start of the war by Lord Krishna, who is an incarnation of Lord Vishnu.

When the war ended after eighteen days, the Pandavas argued over each other's contribution towards their victory.

Bhima said, 'I killed all 100 Kaurava princes, including the mighty Duryodhana. Since he was responsible for this war, killing him makes me the mightiest.'

Arjuna, the third Pandava, said, 'I killed Bhishma who was a mighty warrior. His death was a great blow to the Kauravas. I also killed the valiant Karna. Killing these two killed the morale of our enemies. I think I contributed most to the victory.'

Dhrishtadyumna, Draupadi's brother, said, 'I killed Dronacharya, the teacher of the Pandavas and the Kauravas. That led us to victory.'

Each of the Pandavas boasted of their prowess as the main reason for the victory. To settle their dispute, they went to Krishna.

Krishna said, 'Let us ask Barbarik's head. He watched the whole war from the top of a hill. He also has knowledge of the art of warfare.'

Barbarik laughed and said, 'This is not even a question worth asking. The only person responsible for the victory of the Pandavas is Lord Krishna, the eternal strategist. He killed all those who were not on the side of righteousness.'

Arjuna remembered Lord Krishna had told him the first day when he taught him the Bhagavad Gita that the warriors were already dead and that he (Arjuna) was only a *nimitha*, or a nominal cause, for killing them. Everyone then realised Lord Krishna was the master strategist who guided the Pandavas to victory. It was his strategies that won the war.

He kept Shikhandi in front of Arjun to fight Bhishma. This ensured Bhishma stopped fighting as Shikandi was a woman in his previous life and Bhishma's ethics dictated that he would not fight a woman. Similarly, Drona stopped fighting when Krishna spread a rumour that his son Ashwathama was dead. Krishna also saved Arjuna from the snake dart of Karna. At many critical moments, Krishna guided Arjuna to victory. It was Krishna again who reminded Bhima about the weak spot on Duryodhan's body that Bhima struck to kill him.

The humbled Pandavas expressed gratitude to Lord Krishna. Nature or god does what needs to be done. We are merely instruments in the hands of god or Nature. This awareness creates humility, simplicity and evolution of consciousness.

We may be capable and talented, but if we are egoistical we will have to pay a price. The yaksha is a good example of this.

What leads to greater innovation and quicker evolution?

Even if we are capable of doing things all by ourselves, it is always better to participate in teamwork. Working with others is innovative and leads to self-evolution.

Importance of team effort

One may be capable but cannot be left alone to sort out problems. A combined effort is important for success. The Pandavas worked together and won the war. That was not the case with the Kauravas. Karna, Shakuni and Duryodhana were opposed to Bhishma. Drona, Salya and Karna did not trust each other.

Multiple perspectives, and diverse ideas

Multiple perspectives produce diverse ideas. Diversity, equity and inclusion play a major role in the success of any project. When everyone's contribution is recognised, they feel valued. Every Pandava prince felt he had contributed to their victory.

Teamwork and Inclusion

In tune with Nature

Nature always gets its work done. We are instruments in god's hands, and when participate and cooperate with Nature's plans with that idea, life would not only be simple, easy and fulfilling but also successful.

23

The Unexpected Help

Lord Vishnu's gatekeepers, Jaya and Vijaya, once stopped Lord Brahma's sons, Sanat Kumara and his brothers, from meeting the lord.

In fact, the gatekeepers made fun of the appearance of Brahma's sons, who looked like boys. So, they cursed Jaya and Vijaya for their insolent behaviour: 'Both of you will be reborn on Earth with the qualities of lust, anger and greed.'

During Satya Yuga, Jaya and Vijaya were born as asuras Hiranyakashipu and Hiranyaksha to Sage Kashyapa and his wife Aditi. Hiranyakashipu did penance and prayed to Lord Brahma for immortality. Brahma replied, 'That is impossible.'

Clever Hiranyakashipu then requested, 'I should not die either by man or beast, nor by demons and gods. I should not die during the day or night. I should not die of weapons made of steel, stone or wood. I should not die either indoors or outdoors. I should not die on earth or the sky.'

Brahma had no choice but to grant this boon because his penance was destroying the peace of the cosmos with its heat.

The Unexpected Help

After receiving the boon, Hiranyakashipu plundered Earth. He declared, 'From today, I am to be worshipped as god in my kingdom.'

Earlier, while Hiranyakashipu was in penance, the devas captured his wife, Queen Kayadhu, who was pregnant. The devas planned to kill her as they did not want another asura to be born. However, Sage Narada intervened. He had a divine vision about the unborn baby and its potential to become a great disciple of Lord Vishnu.

Indra allowed Narada to take Queen Kayadhu to his ashram.

Narada was known for giving spiritual discourses about the glory of Lord Vishnu. So Queen Kayadhu listened to all such discourses and meditated along with Narada. Inside her womb, the unborn child also did the same.

When the child was born, he was named Prahlad. By that time, Hiranyakashipu had received his boon, and reached his kingdom and his family joined him there.

However, Prahlad was not like the other asura children. He was serene and virtuous. He educated other asura children in the kingdom to be god-loving and become disciples of Lord Vishnu. When King Hiranyakashipu heard this, he commanded his son to worship him instead.

However, Prahlad did not change. The other asura teachers and elders also tried their best to change Prahlad but nothing worked.

So a frustrated Hiranyakashipu sent a few asuras to kill Prahlad, but they failed. 'Trample him under an elephant,' Hiranyakashipu then ordered. But the elephant was unable to crush the boy.

'Throw him over this cliff,' shouted Hiranyakashipu. But nothing happened to Prahlad.

'Give him poison,' commanded Hiranyakashipu. The poison had no effect on Prahlad.

'Starve him,' said Hiranyakashipu. But Prahlad lived on.

'Use weapons on him,' ordered Hiranyakashipu. Weapons failed to destroy Prahlad. It is said that Lord Vishnu was protecting his devotee.

Hiranyakashipu then asked his sister, Holika, for help. Holika had a special wrap that could protect her against fire. 'Holika, wrap yourself with your special shawl and sit with Prahlad in the fire. He will be burnt to death but you will be saved,' requested Hiranyakashipu.

Holika agreed but just as she and Prahlad sat in the fire, a strong wind blew Holika's shawl away from her shoulders and covered Prahlad's shoulders, protecting him instead. Holika thus burnt to death while Prahlad lived. This day is celebrated as Holika dahan across India.

One day, when Prahlad was engrossed in Lord Vishnu's prayer, Hiranyakashipu challenged Prahlad: 'Where is your god?'

'God is everywhere, Father,' Prahlad replied.

'Is god inside this pillar?' asked Hiranyakashipu, pointing to a nearby pillar.

'Yes,' Prahlad replied.

'Prove it,' an enraged Hiranyakashipu said, hitting the pillar with his mace.

The pillar burst open and out emerged Lord Vishnu as an incarnation of the Narasimha who had the head of a lion and the body of a man. He had the arms and legs of a lion with paws and strong and sharp claws. The clash of Narasimha and Hiranyakashipu was epic. Towards evening, Narsimha dragged Hiranyakashipu towards the doorstep, placed him on his thighs and tore open his belly with his huge sharp claws. Hiranyakashipu died instantly.

So as per Lord Brahma's boon, Hiranyakashipu died neither during day nor night but in the evening. He was killed

The Unexpected Help

by neither man nor god nor animal but by a creature that was half-man and half-lion. He died as a result of the attack by no weapon, metal, wood, or any material, but through the wounds of the claws. Lord Vishnu incarnated as Narasimha and killed Hiranyakashipu according to the conditions laid out in his own boon.

After killing Hiranyakashipu, Narasimha's fury was still high and nobody could calm him down. Then Lord Brahma asked Prahlad to go to Narasimha and seek his blessings. When Prahlad touched the feet of Lord Narasimha, he was instantly pacified. With tender love, Lord Narasimha asked Prahlad, 'Child, ask me for any boon.'

'You are the Lord. What can I ask you? I only want to continue to be in your remembrance and nothing or no one should come in the way of my devotion for you,' Prahlad requested.

Narasimha granted Prahlad his wish.

Narasimha made Prahlad the king of his father's kingdom. 'I will not kill your children, grandchildren or your progeny. Rule wisely and spread the word of god,' instructed Narasimha and left for Vaikuntha.

Despite being an evil asura's son, Prahlad reigned with benevolence and the kingdom prospered under him.

This story teaches us that the education of a child starts in the womb of the mother. Mothers who are benevolent and calm and who meditate and keep their disposition serene and harmonious pass on this noble state to the foetus in their womb. When such a child is born, he or she has the same disposition.

What is the greatest power in the universe?

Sometimes, in spite of great planning, things work out differently. At times when faith in god is strongest, things seem to happen as per Nature's will.

Nobody can outwit nature

Nature cannot be cheated. Death is inevitable. Although Hiranyakashipu was clever in asking for his boon, Nature found a way to outwit him. Hiranyakashipu was killed as per his own boon. Nature is an incredibly powerful force and this story is a reminder of the smallness of our place in the world. It shows the importance of respecting and working in tune with the natural world.

Nature

Nature sends help in unexpected ways

One who has courage and faith in God always receives help from the unknown. While we may not understand why things happen the way they do, we can be assured help may come from unexpected sources when we need it the most.

24

The King Who Knew He Would Die in Seven Days

Parikshit, the son of Abhimanyu and Uttara and the grandson of Arjuna, was the successor of Yudhishthir to the kingdom of Hastinapur.

Parikshit's birth is itself a miraculous story. When he was still in the womb of Uttara, his father Abhimanyu was mercilessly killed by the Kauravas in the Mahabharata war. When Ashwathama of the Kauravas' side learnt of Uttara's unborn child, he attempted to kill it by directing the Brahmastra towards Uttara's womb. Ashwathama wanted to wipe out the Pandavas' lineage as revenge for his father's death. But Uttara was saved by Lord Krishna, who was also the maternal uncle of Abhimanyu. Lord Krishna sent his Sudarshan Chakra to guard Uttara's womb and when the child was stillborn after the war, Krishna brought him back to life through his miraculous yogic powers.

Guru Dhaumya predicted, 'This baby will become one of the greatest disciples of Lord Vishnu and will also be known as

The King Who Knew He Would Die in Seven Days

Vishnurata since he was protected by the lord himself.' He also predicted that Parikshit would be a virtuous, truthful and wise monarch.

When Kali Yuga started, the Pandavas crowned Parikshit and nominated Kripacharya as his tutor.

Kali, the demon who personifies Kali Yuga, once asked Parikshit's permission to inhabit the immoral and unfair areas of his kingdom. Initially, Parikshit denied him entry but when the demon insisted, Parikshit relented. It is said that this demon corrupted Parikshit's mind with anger, impatience and egoism.

Once, Parikshit went hunting and lost his way. He was tired, hungry and thirsty. He stumbled upon Sage Shringi's hut and asked the meditating Sage, 'Oh respected sir, I am dying of thirst. Could you please give me some water?' The Sage was deep in meditation and did not notice the king who asked the Sage for water several times. The king became enraged that he did not get a response, and in anger threw a dead snake around the Sage's neck. Later when the sage's son, Shringi, heard about this incident he felt angry at his father's humiliation and cursed the king, 'I curse him to die of a snakebite seven days from today. Let the most venomous snake, Takshaka, bite him.'

However, the Sage chided his son for the curse as Parikshit was a benevolent king. Shringi felt remorse, but did not have the power to undo his curse. So he informed Parikshit of his impending death.

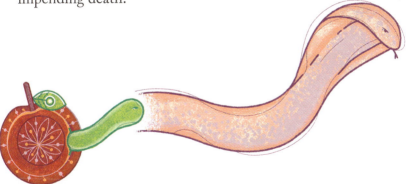

Hearing this, King Parikshit crowned one of his sons, Janamejaya, as the next king and then left, as he desired to spend the last seven days of his life in god's remembrance.

To atone for his action, Parikshit started listening to discourses from Sage Sukhadeva, son of Veda Vyasa. Sage Sukhadeva came to Parikshit on his own to tell him about the great tales of devotion from the *Bhagavata Purana*.

Before listening to the tales of the Lord Vishnu, Parikshit feared death. So, he isolated himself in his palace, built high walls and closed all open spaces and holes. He ensured that no snake could enter his palace. However, after listening to the tales of the devotion of god, his mind became clear and he overcame the fear of death.

Meanwhile, Takshaka, the snake disguised himself as a tiny worm inside a fruit and entered the palace in a vendor's fruit basket. When the king took a bite of that fruit, Takshaka assumed his original form and bit King Parikshit who died immediately. Thus the Sage's curse came true.

Even a great king who is a role model for ethics, integrity and etiquette can lose his temper when unbearably thirsty and commit a mistake. Even though he paid with his life, he was fortunate, for he knew he had exactly seven days to live. Most of us don't know when our end will come. Parikshit spent the last seven days of his life remembering god. He was also lucky to find a spiritual guru like Sukhadeva.

What is the most profound wisdom of our existence?

Live in the present and make the most of it. Focus on what truly matters in life, appreciate the people you love and pursue your dreams and passions.

At the time of death

Both life and death are part of our existence. We cannot run away from this reality. Our consciousness at the time of death may decide what happens to us when we die. The emotions, feelings, ideas, thoughts and attitude that we have when we die prepare us for the journey ahead.

Live As if You Would Die the Next Instant

Live as if you would die the next instant

The feeling of calmness and goodness cannot come instantly. We have to work upon it. Cultivating a lifestyle of harmony, love, brotherhood, nobility, ethical living and compassion may mould our personality in a certain way.

25

Nala Damayanti: A Beautiful Love Story

Once, when Sage Brihadashva visited the Pandavas in exile, Yudhishthir shared with him, 'I feel humiliated and cheated by my cousin, Duryodhana.' To calm and reassure him of better times ahead, Brihadashva told him the love story of Nala and Damayanti.

King Nala was the ruler of Nishadha. A beautiful swan once told him about Damayanti who was the princess of Vidarbha. Fascinated by the description of Damayanti's beauty, Nala asked the swan to tell Damayanti about him too.

Much later, during a swayamvar, an ancient practice where the bride chooses her husband from a group of suitors, Damayanti chose Nala as her husband. Damayanti had heard Nala was an expert in culinary art and a skilled horseman.

When Kali, the evil demon of Kali Yuga, heard the gods praising Nala, he felt angry and jealous. He decided to make Damayanti's life miserable for choosing a mortal over gods.

Kali started looking for flaws in Nala's character and after searching for twelve years, Kali found a small defect in Nala— he often played dice with his brother Pushkara. Kali used this defect to make Nala gamble away his kingdom, wealth and riches. When Nala and Damayanti were forced to leave their kingdom, Damayanti sent her children to her father's kingdom. Under Kali's illusory influence, Nala deserted Damayanti in the forest. As Nala wandered in the jungle, he saw a snake trapped in a fire. The snake was Karkotaka, the son of Sage Kashyapa and Kadru. Nala saved Karkotaka and, as a token of gratitude, Karkotaka transformed Nala into a small ugly dwarf so that he could easily hide in the world.

'Take this magic shawl,' Karkotaka said to Nala. 'When it is time for you to regain your original form, you wrap yourself with this magic garment and you will be back to being Nala again. Until then, go to Ayodhya and serve King Rituparna as a cook and charioteer. He also named Nala as Bahuka, the dwarf. As advised by Karkotaka, Nala got employment in the services of King Rituparna.

Meanwhile, back in the forest, Damayanti was searching for Nala everywhere until finally, she reached Vidarbha, her father's kingdom. She announced a reward to the citizens of Vidarbha: 'Anyone who can help me find my husband will be rewarded with gems, gold and riches.' One day, one of her spies returned with some news.

'There is a dwarf in the kingdom of Ayodhya,' the spy said. 'His name is Bahuka and he is a good chef. He also seems to be good with horses. If he were not a dwarf, I would think he may be Nala.'

Perhaps it is Nala in disguise, thought Damayanti and devised a way to get Nala back. She announced that she would remarry. Hearing this, a shocked Nala disguised as Bahuka came to Vidarbha along with Rituparna.

Damayanti immediately recognised Nala even though he looked like a dwarf. It was then that Nala used the magic garment given by Karkotaka and regained his original form. They were both happy to be reunited.

Rituparna was highly skilled in the game of dice. So Nala asked him for help, 'Teach me to excel in the game. I want to win my kingdom back from my brother.'
In exchange, Rituparna asked Nala, 'Teach me the skills of being an expert horseman and charioteer.'

After they both taught each other their respective skills, Nala rode out to Nishada and challenged his brother. 'Let's have one more game of dice,' Nala said. This time, I pledge the wealth, riches and kingdom inherited by my wife through her father.'

Pushkara was a greedy king and accepted Nala's challenge. But this time Nala was prepared. He was already an expert in dice and so he won the game. Pushkara became a slave of Nala.

'I forgive you. I merely wanted what was rightfully mine.' Saying these words, Nala forgave Pushkara.

By this time, even the demonic Kali was ashamed of his behaviour and sought Nala's forgiveness. After seeking forgiveness from Nala, Kali offered a boon to Nala. Being a wise man, Nala chose judiciously. He knew Kali was the demon of the current time cycle of the universe. So he wisely asked, 'May everyone who read my story be free of Kali's influence. May everyone be pious, wise and not be affected by Kali's demonic powers.'

What is the most precious gift we can give ourselves and others?

> The love story of Nala and Damayanti is inspirational. Such love stories have the ability to transform lives.

Power of love

This story shows the enduring power of love and faith. Damayanti never gives up her love for her husband. He left her because of the illusory mind games of the demon Kali. But she did not give up. Even when Nala lost his kingdom, she stayed by his side. When she saw him as a dwarf, she immediately recognised him. True love remained the same, always.

Everyone transforms in the presence of goodness

There are two beautiful transformational journeys here. Pushkara changes for the better and Nala forgives his brother. The second transformation is even more interesting. The evil demon Kali sought forgiveness from Nala. He realised his folly and repents. Nala forgave him too. What an inspiring transformational agent Nala was!